LET'S PLAY CARDS

GREAT CARD GAMES FOR KIDS!

by
Jude Goodwin

COVER
PHOTOGRAPHY:
LARRY DOELL

**Published by
Devyn Press, Inc.
Louisville, Kentucky**

Other books by Jude Goodwin:

TABLE TALK (Bridge cartoons)
TEACH ME TO PLAY (Bridge for children)

Sometimes the reader is referred to as ''he'' and other times as ''she,''
since both boys and girls will be using this book.

Printed in the United States of America.

Devyn Press, Inc.
151 Thierman Lane
Louisville, KY 40207

ISBN 0-910791-65-1

TABLE OF CONTENTS

CARD GAMES

FUN GAMES

DEDICATION

To my brother, Scott,
who loves cards and
would always play
with his little sister.

And to Brad, for his
help and patience.

CARDS are FUN!

You can build with them, play with them, toss them in the air! You can line them all up, deal them, hold them and hide them.

CARDS CARDS CARDS. They are small, they are neat. They are like a little book. You can play cards with your friends. You can play cards by yourself. Cards are for games. Cards are for magic. Cards are for FUN!

Kids can play cards with their brothers and sisters, with their mommys and daddys, even the babysitter. People play cards every day, all over the world...
CARDS are AMAZING!
All this FUN
   in one little pile...

5

LET'S LOOK at the CARDS

Spread your deck of cards out on the table...

In each deck there are 4 SUITS

 SPADES HEARTS DIAMONDS  CLUBS

Each suit has 13 cards

ACE KING QUEEN JACK

The A K Q and J are called HONOR CARDS. I guess this is because they look like a ROYAL FAMILY! There's an A K Q and J in each suit.

10 9 8 7 6 5 4 3 2

These are called SPOT CARDS because they are covered with spots.

Count the number of SPOTS in the middle of a SPOT CARD. It is the same as the number on the card!

A MAGIC KINGDOM

Each of the 4 suits is like a KINGDOM of CARDS!

Aces are like Presidents and in most games, the Ace is the highest card in a suit.

Then the KING is the ruler of the kingdom and is the 2ND highest card in a suit.

The QUEEN rules by his side and is the 3RD highest card in a suit.

The JACK, their son, is the 4TH highest card.

All the SPOT CARDS are the kingdom's subjects and stand in the kingdom according to their RANK.
The TEN is the highest spot card and has the most spots! Then the 9 and the 8 and so on — right down to the little 2...

10 9 8 7 6 5 4 3 2

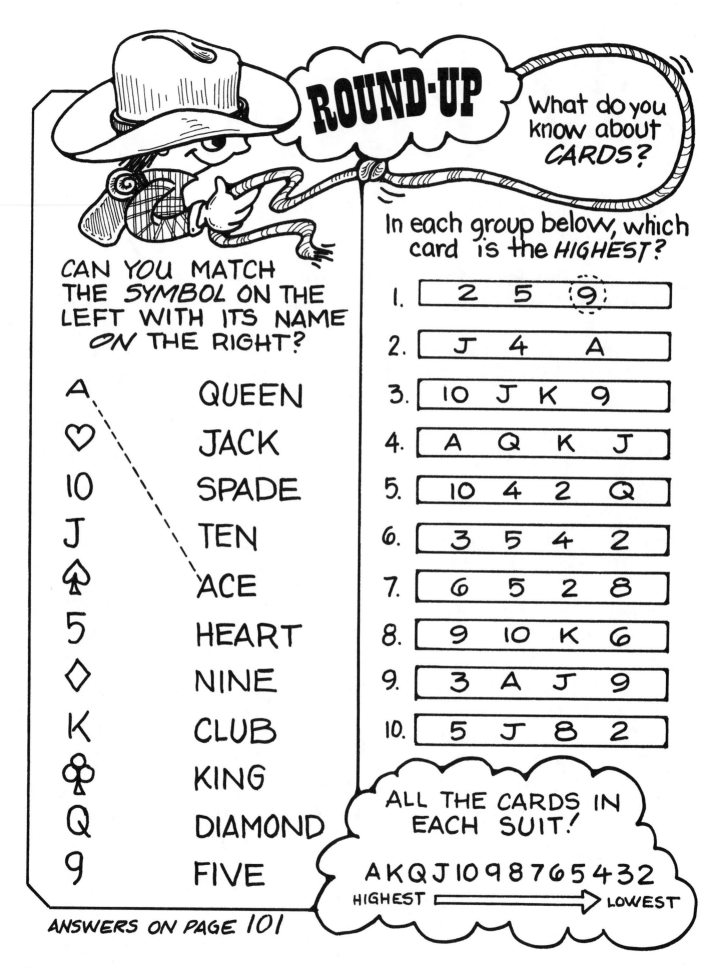

ROUND-UP

What do you know about *CARDS?*

CAN *YOU* MATCH THE *SYMBOL* ON THE LEFT WITH ITS NAME *ON* THE RIGHT?

A
♥
10
J
♠
5
◇
K
♣
Q
9

QUEEN
JACK
SPADE
TEN
ACE
HEART
NINE
CLUB
KING
DIAMOND
FIVE

In each group below, which card is the *HIGHEST?*

1. | 2 | 5 | (9) |
2. | J | 4 | A |
3. | 10 | J | K | 9 |
4. | A | Q | K | J |
5. | 10 | 4 | 2 | Q |
6. | 3 | 5 | 4 | 2 |
7. | 6 | 5 | 2 | 8 |
8. | 9 | 10 | K | 6 |
9. | 3 | A | J | 9 |
10. | 5 | J | 8 | 2 |

ALL THE CARDS IN EACH SUIT!

A K Q J 10 9 8 7 6 5 4 3 2

HIGHEST ⟶ LOWEST

ANSWERS ON PAGE 101

THE DEALER

The dealer is the person who gives out all the cards.

TAKE TURNS BEING THE DEALER

HOW TO PICK THE FIRST DEALER
Spread the cards faces down, on the table.
Everyone picks one card and turns it over.
The person who picks the highest card is first dealer.
If there is a TIE, those two pick again.
After the FIRST DEAL, the player to the
LEFT of the DEALER deals next.

ALWAYS DEAL THE CARDS FACE DOWN

Each person's cards are his SECRET!

DEAL THE CARDS ONE AT A TIME

Make sure you don't show a card's face by mistake. If you do, put it in the middle of the deck and deal another...

ALWAYS DEAL TO THE LEFT

Start by dealing the first card to the player on DEALER'S LEFT. Then the next player, then the next— all around the table. Dealer gives herself a card LAST.

TAKING TURNS

In almost ALL card games, the players TAKE TURNS.

Unless the rules say something different, the person on dealer's LEFT goes FIRST.

Then the person on that person's LEFT goes next. And so on...

ALWAYS REMEMBER WHOSE TURN IT IS!

SHUFFLE

Before each deal, you have to SHUFFLE the cards. Shuffling the cards will mix them up so they aren't in any special order.

THE EASIEST SHUFFLE
to do is this:

Spread all the cards, FACE DOWN, on the table and MIX THEM UP. Mix and Mix. Then gather them up and form them back into a tidy deck.

The CUT SHUFFLE

Put the deck on the table. Take off about half the deck and make a second pile. Then, pick up the bottom part and put it on top. Do this over and over until the deck is good and mixed!

The PUSH SHUFFLE

If your hands are clever, you can cut the deck into 2 piles and then push them together so they mix. Hold the two piles LOOSELY so the cards can slide between each other.

WAR!

YOUR FIRST CARD GAME

Deal each player a card, starting with the player on dealer's left. Deal the cards with their FACES DOWN.

⭐ NOBODY LOOKS AT THEIR CARDS – *OK?*

Keep dealing cards to each player until all the cards are dealt. Everyone will have a pile of cards in front of them FACING DOWN.

★ ★ Starting with the person on dealer's left, each player turns over ONE card and puts it in the middle of the table – FACE UP... ★ ★

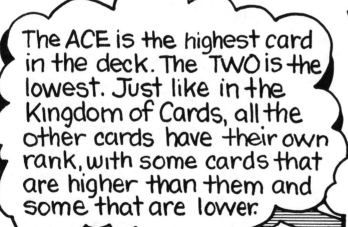

The ACE is the highest card in the deck. The TWO is the lowest. Just like in the Kingdom of Cards, all the other cards have their own rank, with some cards that are higher than them and some that are lower.

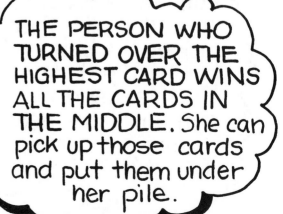

THE PERSON WHO TURNED OVER THE HIGHEST CARD WINS ALL THE CARDS IN THE MIDDLE. She can pick up those cards and put them under her pile.

IF THERE IS A
☆ TIE ☆
FOR HIGHEST
CARD THEN THE
PLAYERS WHOSE
CARDS ARE 'TIED'
MUST GO TO
WAR

A TIE means two or more people played a card with the same RANK. If this happens with the HIGHEST card, the players must GO TO WAR to see who wins the pile!

Each of the TIED players plays 3 more cards FACE DOWN in the middle and then ONE FACE UP. The highest of *these* face up cards wins all the cards in the middle. If *these* cards are *also* TIED, then the players each play 5 *more* cards FACE DOWN and ONE FACE UP. This keeps going on, adding 2 to the number of FACE DOWN cards until someone WINS THE WAR *and ALL the MIDDLE cards!*

This game is played until someone has won ALL the cards in the DECK. *Then, that person is the* WINNER!

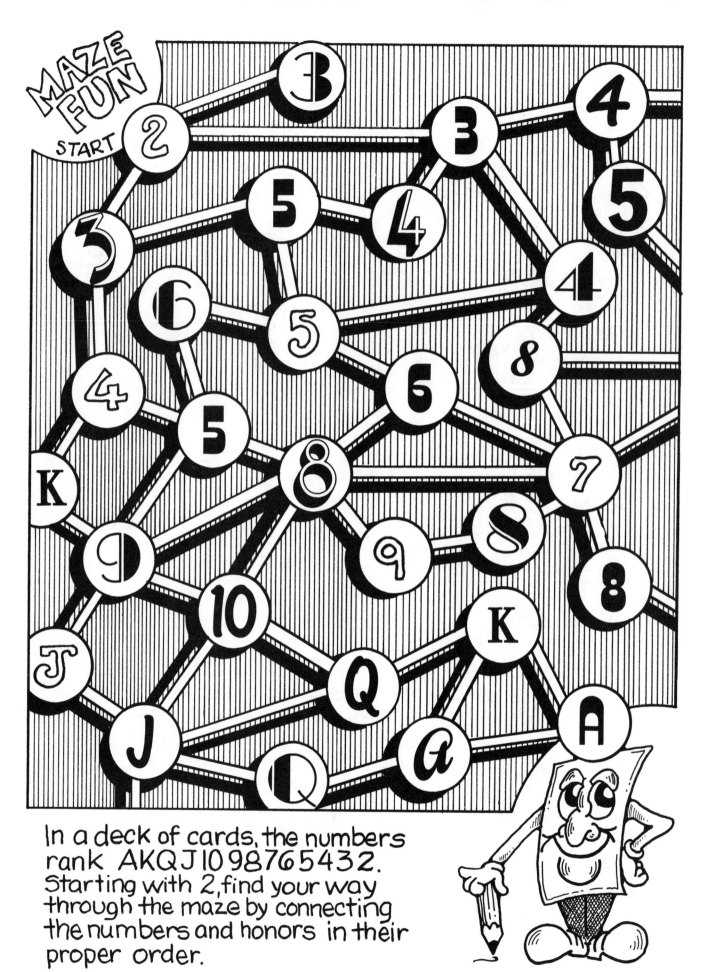

In a deck of cards, the numbers rank AKQJ10987654 32. Starting with 2, find your way through the maze by connecting the numbers and honors in their proper order.

Wouldn't it be fun to have a card party.!?
You can ask your Mom or Dad if it
would be all right to have some friends
over to play cards!

Be sure to pick a time when no one in
the house is sleeping!

You don't need tables. You can play on the
floor. You just need some cushions.

CARD PARTY IDEAS

PRIZES

You might want to give prizes to the winners of each game! Here are some ideas...

☆ Buy an extra bag of balloons and DON'T BLOW THEM UP. Give one to each winner... kind of like ribbons on SPORTS DAY!

OR

☆ Buy a box of cookies. Give one to the winners. At the end of the party you can give out what cookies are left! m.m..

INVITATIONS

If you have some OLD cards lying around, you can paste a piece of paper over the SPOTS and write you invitation on the paper... Your invitations will be like CARDS!

OR If you don't have any old cards, you can trace around a card on heavy paper and draw the invitation to LOOK like a card!

You can all play the same game or you can divide into groups and play different games.

good games
SNAP
ANIMALS
SOCKS
GO FISH

You are INVITED! to a CARD PARTY ♡ ♤ ♧ ♢ SUNDAY 1:00 PM My Place BRING YOUR CARDS

GO FISH

This is a fun game for 2 or more players.

THE DEAL

If there are 2 players, deal 7 cards to each player. If there are more than 2 players, deal 5 cards to each player.

Put the rest of the cards FACE DOWN in the middle. This is THE PILE.

Hold your cards so that ONLY YOU can see their FACES.

The cards you are holding are called your HAND

The person to the left of the dealer is first. This is how you play...

When it's your turn, you ask ANY OTHER PLAYER if they have a certain card. Like a 10 or a King or a 3. If the player you asked has one or more of that card, he must GIVE THEM ALL TO YOU. If this happens, you can then ask another player for a different card. Or, you can ask the same player. Or you can ask someone else for the same card!

4 OF A KIND

What you are trying to do is collect SETS of 4 cards, all of the same RANK. Like 4 3s or 4 Queens or 4 Aces. You ask players for cards that will help you get 4 of a kind. When you get 4 of a kind, you put them down in front of you. The first person to get rid of all the cards in his hand **WINS!** He got rid of his cards by putting them down in sets of 4 of a kind.

If the person you ask doesn't have the card you asked for, she says **"GO" Fish**

When someone tells you to GO FISH, you draw one card from the top of THE PILE

If the card you draw from the PILE is the same as the one you asked for, you say∘○? ...and your turn starts all over!

GOT WHAT I ASKED FOR!

If the card you draw is NOT what you asked for, YOUR TURN IS OVER. Now its the person on your LEFT'S turn.

IF the PILE runs out, the game is over and the person with the most 4 of a kinds will be the WINNER.

RULE

YOU MUST HAVE A CARD IN YOUR HAND THAT IS THE SAME AS THE ONE YOU ASKED FOR. You can't ask for a card unless you have one like it in your hand.
HAVE FUN!

SNAP!

The game of SNAP is lots of fun at parties but watch out... SNAP is LOUD!

HOW TO DEAL

HOW TO PLAY

Deal the cards FACE DOWN in front of each player. *PLAYERS DO NOT LOOK AT THEIR CARDS!* Keep dealing until all the cards are dealt. There will be a pile of cards in front of each player.

Taking turns, you each turn over the top card of your pile and put it in front of you. This starts your SNAP PILE. You must turn up your card AWAY from you so so you don't see it before everyone else. *Turn your cards up quickly!*

When a card turned up matches a card on someone else's SNAP PILE, the first of those two players to yell SNAP! wins both SNAP PILES. The loser starts the play again. If you yell SNAP! at the wrong time, you have to give every player one card.

The person who wins ALL THE CARDS is the WINNER!

ANIMALS

This game is the same as SNAP to play, but with ONE FUNNY DIFFERENCE!

Deal the cards and play like SNAP BUT FIRST...

Everyone chooses to be an animal. You can be a cow or a goat or a dog or anything...

When, during the play, 2 cards match, instead of saying *SNAP*, each person must make the sound of the other person's animal! The person who makes the right sound FIRST wins both SNAP PILES.

If both make the wrong sound, no one wins the PILES.
If one makes the wrong sound he must give one card from his face down pile to the person who won his SNAP PILE.
If a person makes an animal sound at the wrong time, he must give a card to whoever is that animal.

OINK!

QUACK!

MEOW

BAA-A

WHO-O-O

Starting with 2, connect the dots in the order of cards and draw the hidden pictures!

2 3 4 5 6 7 8 9 10 J Q K A

DOT to DOT its easy!

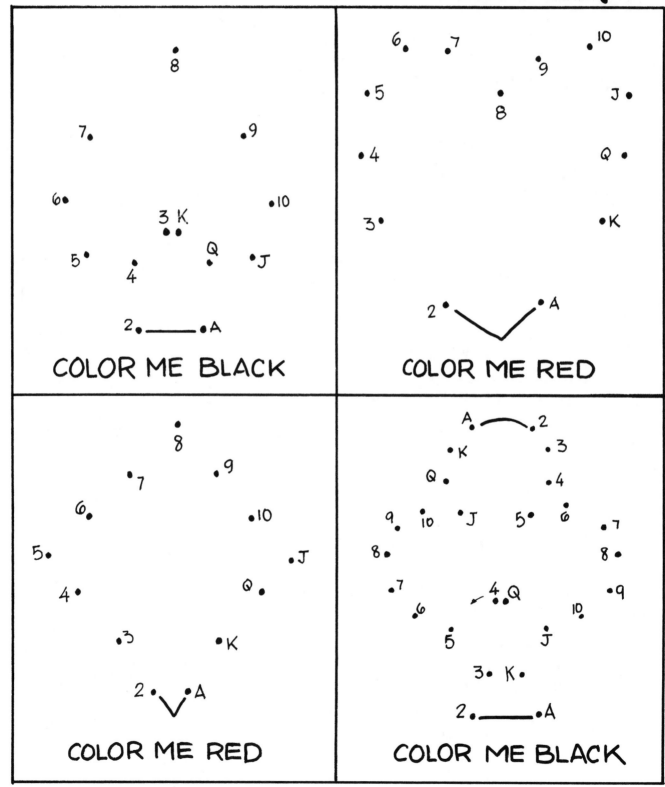

COLOR ME BLACK

COLOR ME RED

COLOR ME RED

COLOR ME BLACK

SOCKS

This game is

FAST!
FUN
and FRANTIC!

GET READY

Go through the DECK and pick out SETS of 4 OF A KIND. Pick out as many sets as there are people playing. Put all the rest of the cards away.

NOW SHUFFLE the SETS of 4 of a kind together. Shuffle WELL so that all the sets are MIXED TOGETHER!

You'll need to ask your Mom or Dad for some SOCKS! Roll these up like you do when they come out of the laundry. Make them into soft little balls. You can ask a big person to help...

GET SET

Everyone sits in a circle. In the middle, you put ONE LESS SOCK than there are people playing.

FOR EXAMPLE → If there are 5 people playing, put 4 sock-balls in the middle. If there are 4 people playing, put 3 sock balls in the middle.

Dealer takes the shuffled pile of cards and deals 4 cards, FACE DOWN, to each player. Players hold these cards so that ONLY THEY can see them.

SOMEONE SAYS GO!

Players start passing cards to the person on their left. Pass ANY card, one at a time, FACE DOWN. Meanwhile, you pick up cards being passed to you!

This all happens at once.
PASS AND PICK UP! PASS AND PICK UP!

AS SOON AS SOMEONE GETS 4 OF A KIND, HE PUTS HIS CARDS FACE UP ON THE FLOOR AND GRABS A SOCK! When this happens, EVERYONE grabs a sock. The last person to grab a sock will lose because there will be NO SOCKS LEFT!

KEEP SCORE °°° Everyone gets I point except the loser. Before you start, decide how many games you'll play. In the end, the person with the most points WINS!

CONCENTRATION

Play this card game with as many people as you want. You will need to play on a large table, or better yet, a floor.

SPREAD OUT ALL THE CARDS IN ONE DECK. SPREAD THEM *FACE DOWN* IN FRONT OF EVERYBODY.

Taking turns, each player turns over 2 cards, without changing their position. If the 2 cards MATCH as a pair (2 of a kind) you pick them up and pile them in front of you AND take another turn. If the 2 cards DON'T MATCH, you turn them back *FACE DOWN* and it is the next person's turn.

At the end of the game, when all the cards are gone, the person with the MOST pairs WINS.

HINT Watch what cards the other players turn over and where they are! This game is called CONCENTRATION because you must *THINK* and *REMEMBER* where the cards are!

FIND-A-WORD

Here is a fun pencil puzzle for you to do! First, pick a word from the list. Then find that word in the box of jumbled letters. Draw a circle around the word. We have done one for you as an example. The words may run up, down, sideways, forward, backward, or on a slant. Any letter may be used more than once!

```
A Q E T W I S T Q
C U U O H E T S U
E E T E N R N E E
I F I V E I E V E
G O I A K N O E P
H U J C S I X N G
T R A M S N N S N
A J C E A E O D I
C E T T W O D P K
```

WORD LIST

ACE
KING
QUEEN
~~JACK~~
TEN
NINE
EIGHT
SEVEN
SIX
FIVE
FOUR
THREE
TWO

CROSS THE WORDS
OUT AS YOU
FIND THEM...

Answers on page 101

26

I DOUBT IT

This is a *great* party game!
Up to 12 people can play.
It is good and noisy AND
you are expected to cheat!

deal

Deal out ALL the cards, face down.
  If you have more than 5 players, you
  will need 2 decks.
Players hold their cards so that only
  they can see them.

Remember to *take turns* being DEALER.

The player to the LEFT of DEALER goes FIRST!

play

FIRST PLAYER PLAYS ACES
  She takes a number of cards from her hand,
  places them *FACE DOWN* on the table and
  DECLARES how many ACES she has played.
  She might say
    "3 Aces" or "4 Aces"!
  She can DECLARE as *many* as she wants,
  up to 4 if there is one deck or 8 if there
  are 2 decks of cards in play.

SECOND PLAYER PLAYS KINGS.
THIRD PLAYER PLAYS QUEENS.
The next player plays JACKS. The next,
TENS. This goes on around and around
the table   *IN ORDER.*

A K Q J 10 9 8 7 6 5 4 3 2

The player after 2s starts over
again with ACES.

Each player, in turn, takes some
number of cards from her hand and
puts them *FACE DOWN* on the table.
She DECLARES how many cards she
played and what RANK it is.

IT IS VERY IMPORTANT
that you play all your cards
FACE DOWN!

BECAUSE YOU COULD BE
CHEATING or *FOOLING!*

Sometimes, you *WON'T HAVE ANY CARDS*
in the RANK you must put down.
When this happens, you will have to put
down some *other* cards and LIE!

Because the cards are *FACE DOWN,*
no one can be sure whether you
are lying or not.

IN THIS GAME IT IS O.K. TO LIE,
CHEAT, OR TRY TO FOOL THE OTHERS!

in order

FUN part

IF YOU THINK THE PERSON WHO LAST DECLARED IS LYING *or* CHEATING, YOU SAY

I doubt it!

Any player can say "I DOUBT IT!" after any DECLARER. Then, you turn over the cards to see if the DECLARER was *FOOLING YOU!*

If he was, he must pick up the ENTIRE PILE.

after an "I DOUBT IT" play goes on...

If he was TELLING the TRUTH, the person who said "I DOUBT IT" must pick up the ENTIRE PILE!

If 2 or more people say "I DOUBT IT!" at the same time, the one closest to DECLARER'S LEFT is the official doubter. Otherwise, the person who says "I DOUBT IT!" FIRST is the doubter.

If someone says "I DOUBT IT" before a player has DECLARED their cards, that call is ignored and the doubter can't call again until the next person's turn.

THE PLAYER WHO GETS RID OF ALL THE CARDS IN HIS HAND *FIRST* IS THE

WINNER

Here are some HINTS to help you become an EXPERT "I DOUBT IT" player!

PLAN AHEAD! You can tell, by counting around the table, what cards you must put down on your turns. Try to keep some TRUE CARDS for later in the game!

REMEMBER HOW MANY CARDS THERE ARE IN THE DECK!

THERE ARE 4 OF EACH RANK IN ONE DECK.

Now, if you have 2 8s in your hand, say, and someone tries to DECLARE 3 8s, you KNOW he is LYING!
2+3=5 and there are ONLY 4 in the DECK!

If there are 2 DECKS, there are 8 of each RANK in the DEAL.

It helps to look at what cards were played when someone has to turn some over.

Try to KEEP COUNT if you can.

As the game goes on, it gets *harder and harder* to TELL THE TRUTH!

This is because *MOST* of the cards have been played. Chances are good that people won't have the cards they are supposed to play!

Players say I DOUBT IT more at the END of a game than at the beginning...

It's a GOOD IDEA to CHEAT EARLY! and save your TRUE CARDS for later in the game. Very likely, noone will DOUBT you.

AND unless you are SURE, don't start saying "I DOUBT IT" until a few rounds have been played.

Watch people's FACES! Do they look GUILTY? *and* what about *YOUR FACE*!?
Try to keep a straight face....don't give yourself away!

DON'T BE SILLY! Don't try to put down too many cards at one time...someone is *SURE* to say "I DOUBT IT!", bub!

You can *also* lie about the *number* of cards you put down! You can *say* 3 but really put down 4 or 5 cards...

CRAZY EIGHTS!

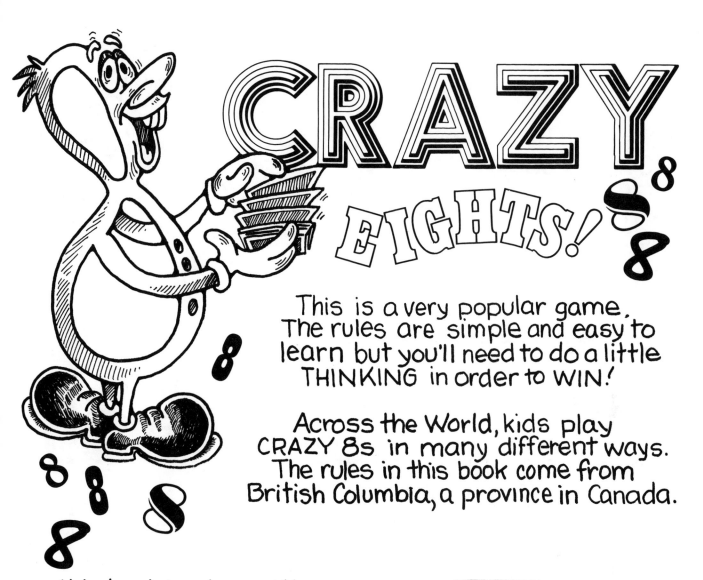

This is a very popular game. The rules are simple and easy to learn but you'll need to do a little THINKING in order to WIN!

Across the World, kids play CRAZY 8s in many different ways. The rules in this book come from British Columbia, a province in Canada.

It is best to play with 2, 3 or 4 players. Deal 8 cards to each player, FACE DOWN. The players hold their cards so only they can see them.

Put the remaining cards FACE DOWN in the middle of the table. This is the PILE.

Turn over the TOP card of the PILE and put it FACE UP next to the Pile. This starts the DISCARD PILE.

PILE
face down

DISCARD PILE
face up

The way to win this game is to DISCARD or get rid of all the cards in your hand by playing them on the DISCARD PILE. Each turn you may play one card on the DISCARD PILE **BUT** it must MATCH the TOP CARD of the Discard Pile in either SUIT or RANK!

LOOK

If the top card of the DISCARD PILE is the 7♡ you can play ANY 7 *(same rank)* or ANY ♡ *(same suit)*. If the top card was the 10◇, you could play ANY 10 or ANY ◇.

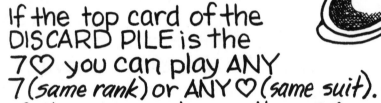 SAME RANK ᴏʀ SAME SUIT!

If you cannot DISCARD because you don't have a card that matches the DISCARD PILE, then you must DRAW, or TAKE one card from the face down PILE and add it to your hand.

The first person to DISCARD all the cards in his hand is the **WINNER**

In CRAZY 8s there are some
SPECIAL CARDS!

8 IS WILD! You can play ANY 8 on the DISCARD PILE and change the suit to ANYTHING YOU WANT.. You can play an 8 even if it doesn't match. All these other SPECIAL CARDS must be the same suit or rank as the face up card.

2 IS NASTY! If you play any 2, the next person to play must pick up 2 cards before he starts his turn.

Q OF SPADES If you play the QUEEN of SPADES, the next person to play must pick up 5 cards before he takes his turn.

J MISS A TURN If you play ANY Jack, the next person must MISS A TURN.

K REVERSE If you play a King, the order of turns is REVERSED. The play will go to the right, instead of the left. Another King changes it back.

last card When you have only one card left, you must say "LAST CARD". If you don't say this, or if someone else sees you're on your last card and says it first, you pick up 8 CARDS!

BUILDING
With Cards!

Someday, you might be just sitting around on the carpet, playin' with your cards, not much on your mind ... you could try building a card house! Carpets and rugs are best because their threads help the cards stand up AND no one will come by and jiggle them. A table might get *bumped* and your house of cards will tumble down! Here is one idea for starting a card house ...

①

Place cards here to keep upright cards from sliding.

②

Lean Wall cards here

③ Set Roof cards on top

RUMMY

Rummy is one of the world's best loved games. It is played by people of all ages and all nationalities. In some countries, Rummy is played with tiles instead of cards.

In Rummy, the players can keep a score. People who play lots of Rummy sometimes keep a score that runs over days and weeks. They just add to the score every time they meet. You and your friends will find Rummy EASY TO LEARN and a good game to play.

Big people like to play RUMMY too!

After you have learned to play, ask your grandfather for a game!

Or your Dad
  Or your Mom
    Or your Aunt
      OR
      ANYONE!

You and your friends will have FUN playing

RUMMY!

THE ♡ DEAL

You can play RUMMY with 2, 3, 4, 5 or 6 players.

If there are 2 players, deal 10 cards to each.
If there are 3 or 4, deal 7 cards.
If there are 5 or 6, deal 6 cards.

Put the rest of the cards face down in a pile in the middle. This is called the STOCK.
Take the top card from the STOCK and put it face up next to the STOCK.
This starts the DISCARD PILE.

Hold your cards in your hand so that only you can see them.

FACE DOWN STOCK PILE

FACE UP DISCARD PILE

THE PLAY

What you try to do in the play is collect SETS. There are 2 kinds of SETS.

⟹ A GROUP of 3 or 4 cards of the SAME RANK.
  like 3 Jacks or 4 Aces or 3 fours....
⟹ A SEQUENCE of 3 or more cards in the SAME SUIT
  like 2, 3, 4 of ♠ or J Q K A of ♡ or 9 10 J of ♣

Read the next page to find out how to collect these SETS!

MORE!

ITS EASY

Players at RUMMY take turns. Each turn has 3 PARTS.

PART 1
You DRAW a card. You can draw *(pick up)* a card from the top of the STOCK or the top of the DISCARD PILE.

PART 2
After you have drawn a card, you can put down any SETS that you have. You put these SETS down FACE UP in front of you. BUT you don't HAVE to put sets down.
You can also ADD CARDS to SOMEONE ELSE'S SETS *as long as they match* either the sequence or rank.

PART 3
You END your TURN by throwing a card away on the DISCARD PILE. *This is called DISCARDING.*

If you are playing only one game, the first person to use up all his cards and GO OUT is the WINNER! When playing more than one game you will want to learn to *SCORE!*

GOING OUT...

The game is over when someone GOES OUT by putting all his cards into sets. If the DRAW at the beginning of a turn lets a player turn all his cards into SETS, he doesn't have to DISCARD. But he may also GO OUT by putting down all his cards but one. This last card he can DISCARD.

what's the SCORE?

Take a piece of paper. Across the top, write the names of everyone who is playing. You will write each person's score, for each hand, in a column under his name.

When someone GOES OUT, the hand is over and everyone adds up his score.

At the bottom of this page you will see how many points each card is worth. Subtract the number of points in your hand from the number of points on the table in front of you. That is your SCORE. If you have more points in your hand than you do on the table, you will get a MINUS score. This MINUS score will be subtracted from your next score. You got a MINUS score because you kept too many cards in your HAND! When you are playing, if it looks like someone is close to GOING OUT, try to put down as many cards as you can so you will end up with a PLUS SCORE!

	Ziggy	Luke	Ashley
			50
		40	30
HAND 1	85	35	
HAND 2	45		80
		75	20
TOTAL	130	50	
HAND 3	-10		100
		125	20
TOTAL	120	90	
HAND 4	30		120
TOTAL	150	215	

Here are the number of points each card COUNTS

ACE   15 POINTS
K·Q·J·10   10 POINTS
ALL OTHERS   5 POINTS

RUMMY

SOME RULES and NOTES

↱ When you ADD a card to someone else's SET, you POINT to their SET, but you put your card in front of you. This way, the card earns you points, not the other player!

↱ If you use up the STOCK, just shuffle up the DISCARD pile and turn it over. BUT, be sure to keep the top card of the old discard pile to start the new discard pile.

↱ You can NEVER *look through* the DISCARD PILE. You see ONLY the top card.

↱ ## "RUMMY"

If someone DISCARDS a card that could have been played on a SET, *ANYONE* can say "RUMMY!" and pick up that card. He then plays it where it should go and DISCARDS from his hand. After this, the 'turn' goes back to where it is supposed to be...

TIPS

You don't want to put your SETS down too soon. Other players may be able to use up their cards sooner by adding to your SETS. BUT - you don't want to hold onto your sets *too long* either, especially HIGH POINT sets like A·A·A· or AKQJ. You might get *STUCK* when someone GOES OUT.

WILD?

Some people like to play that 2s are WILD and can be used as ANY rank or suit. WILD 2s count as 20 points. AND, you can TRADE a 2 for the card it is meant to be. *For example,* if someone uses a 2 instead of the 10♡, if YOU have the 10♡, when it is your turn you can put your card in their set and
TAKE THE 2!

CUT THE DECK

When you play cards, you will often be asked to *CUT the DECK*...

Sometimes, after the DEALER has shuffled, she will ask the player on her right to *CUT*. This is to make sure the bottom card is buried in the middle. *(in case someone saw it!)* Many card tricks, too, need someone to *CUT the DECK*.

HOW TO *CUT THE DECK!*

① PICK UP PART OF THE DECK *(about half).*

② PUT IT NEXT TO THE BOTTOM HALF SO THERE ARE 2 PILES...

③ BOTTOM CARD

NOW PICK UP THE BOTTOM HALF AND PUT IT ON TOP!

④ BOTTOM CARD

WHEN THE *CUT* IS FINISHED, THE DECK IS WHOLE AGAIN *and* THE BOTTOM CARD IS BURIED.

You can *CUT THE DECK* in order to choose who is dealer. Simply *CUT* and look at the card! Most of the time, highest card deals. You can *CUT* wherever you want in the Deck, but there should always be *at least 4 cards* in either the TOP or BOTTOM half.

Just for **FUN!**

Some people can cut the deck while holding it in one hand! This is *HARD* to do and takes a lot of PRACTICE...

HOLD THE DECK AS HIGH UP ON YOUR FINGER TIPS AND THUMB TIPS AS YOU CAN...

BEND YOUR THUMB A BIT AND LET THE BOTTOM HALF FALL INTO YOUR PALM.

SIDE VIEW

NOW SLIDE YOUR POINTER FINGER UNDER THE BOTTOM HALF AND PUSH IT TOWARDS YOUR THUMB

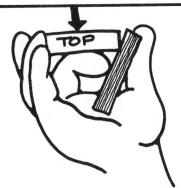

THE BOTTOM HALF IS NOW RESTING BETWEEN YOUR THUMB AND THE TOP HALF. THE TOP HALF RESTS ON YOUR POINTER FINGER.

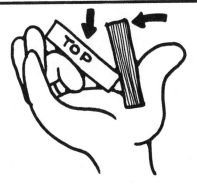

START LOWERING YOUR POINTER FINGER. THE TOP HALF BEGINS TO SLIDE DOWN. THE OTHER HALF WANTS TO FALL ON TOP!

AS THIS HAPPENS, CLOSE YOUR HAND. THE BOTTOM HALF FALLS ON THE TOP AND VOILA! THE DECK IS CUT! AND WHOLE AGAIN...

41

NINETY NINE

This is a quick and easy adding game with special cards and strategy!

99 can be played with 2,3,4 or 5 players. Deal 3 cards to each. Players hold their cards so that only they can see them.

Put the rest of the cards in the middle of the table, FACE DOWN. This is the STOCK PILE.

The first player takes a card from his hand and places it, FACE UP, next to the STOCK PILE. This starts the ADDING PILE. He must call out the card's VALUE as he does this. Then he takes a card from the STOCK.

The next player puts a card from his hand on top of the ADDING PILE and, adding it to the card below, calls out the TOTAL. Then he draws a card from the STOCK.

The next player plays a card and, ADDING it to the TOTAL, calls out the NEW total. Then she draws a card.

The play keeps going, each player adding the VALUE of their card to the TOTAL

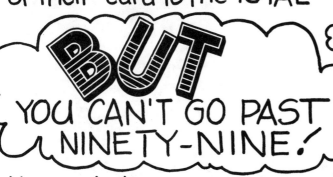

BUT

YOU CAN'T GO PAST NINETY-NINE!

You can't play a card whose value will make the TOTAL more than 99!
If you cannot play a card, you say PASS.
If you say PASS 3 turns in a row, you are OUT.
The last person in the game is the WINNER!

the VALUE of the cards

K Equals ZERO. Play the King when the TOTAL is 99, and it will stay 99.

10 Subtract 10. Play the Ten and the TOTAL becomes 10 less than it was.

9 Makes the TOTAL equal 99. Even if it is the first card played, the total will go to 99. If the total is already 99, the 9 makes it stay at 99.

4 REVERSE the order of play. The 4 does not add to the total. If the play was moving to the left, the 4 makes it move to the right. Another 4 would change it back to the left again.

AND

ACES equal One. Q and J equal Ten. OTHER CARDS equal their number.

Strategy!
Save your Special Cards if you can. You will want to use them when the TOTAL equals 99!

Use your REVERSE card when the player, whose turn was before you, said PASS. A 4 card will make it his turn again and he will have to say PASS again!

CARD MAGIC

You can amaze your friends with these card tricks!

Many card tricks have someone choose a card, remember it, then bury it in the deck.

As the MAGICIAN, you then FIND that card in a most *amazing* way!

This kind of card trick has 2 parts.

1 Secretly find the chosen card in a way not known to your audience.

2 Perform a magical *ENDING* to the trick where you find the card in a seemingly *IMPOSSIBLE* way.

MAGICIANS' LAWS

① NEVER perform a trick more than twice in front of the same audience.

② NEVER reveal your *SECRET!* However, many magicians *TRADE* their secrets among themselves.

Here are some different ways to *SECRETLY* find out what card a spectator has *CHOSEN*.

Once you know the CHOSEN CARD, you can perform one of the *Magical Endings*.

the KEY CARD METHOD

Shuffle the deck. Put it on the table. Cut the deck, and hold the top half in your hand. Point to the half on the table and ask the spectator to look at the top card and *MEMORIZE* it.

MEANWHILE, *SECRETLY* look at the card on the BOTTOM of the half you hold in your hand. You can do this when you point at the pack on the table, because the spectator will be looking where you are pointing. *This is the KEY CARD!*

Now ask the spectator to replace the chosen card on top of the pack. You put your half on top.

When this is done, the KEY CARD will be directly on TOP of the Chosen Card. Now, even though you don't know *WHAT* the chosen card is, you know *WHERE* it is in the deck. It will be right after the KEY CARD.

TOP HALF

YOUR KEY CARD

CHOSEN CARD

45

the Picture Book METHOD

This trick can only be done with a deck of cards that has pictures on its backs - like horses, or boats - rather than a design.

PREPARE THE DECK!
Before you do this trick, you must sort the deck so that ALL THE PICTURES FACE THE SAME WAY.

Of course, you want to do this without anyone noticing! It is actually easy to do while people are talking. It just looks like you are fidgeting with the cards. *DO THIS BEFORE YOU SAY YOU ARE GOING TO DO A TRICK!*

CARD BACKS FACE THE SAME WAY

TURN DECK AROUND

You can shuffle or cut the deck but *DO NOT REVERSE* any cards!

You or Spectator cut the deck into 2 packs. Spectator looks at the card on top of one pack and replaces it. While he does this, you pick up the other pack and TURN IT AROUND. Don't look down as you do this!

CHOSEN CARD

the chosen card
Go through the deck, looking ONLY AT THE BACKS! (This will impress those in your audience who know the KEY CARD method!) When the cards *REVERSE DIRECTION* you know the FIRST REVERSED CARD is the CHOSEN CARD.

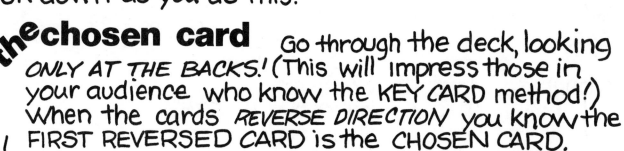

WATCH!

Sometimes, a SPECTATOR will unknowingly reverse the CHOSEN CARD before replacing it! Now, you simply pick up the other pack and place it on top. The one reversed card is the CHOSEN CARD!

PART 2 MAGICAL ENDINGS

Once you have figured out *WHERE* the chosen card is, *CUT* the deck so it is *ON THE TOP.*

Do this in a clever way so your audience doesn't know!

KEY CARD
☆ Hold the deck so you are looking at the faces of the cards.
☆ Pretend you are trying to guess the card as you go through the deck looking for your KEY CARD.
☆ When you find the KEY CARD, *PRETEND TO CHANGE YOUR MIND.* Say something like "I'll tell you what I'll do..." or "This isn't working..." *AT THE SAME TIME* cut the deck at the KEY CARD so the chosen Card is on the Top. If you talk suddenly, while you cut, the audience will look at *YOU*, not at your hands!

PICTURE BOOK
Just go through the deck in your hands and *casually cut it* where the cards REVERSE!

HAT TRICK

COWBOY HATS ARE GOOD TOO!

You need a HAT that is *STIFF* and has a *DENT* in the top...

As you *CUT* the deck, *distract* your audience by asking someone to get the HAT. Turn the hat over and *HOLD IT HIGH.* Put the deck *IN THE HAT,* but make sure the *CHOSEN CARD* falls on one side of the *ridge inside,* and the rest are on the other side.

CHOSEN CARD

HAT

NOW If you HIT the bottom of the hat, the chosen Card will *FLY OUT!*

SMASH!

STRIKE DOWN!

CHOSEN CARD

You will have FUN with this magical ending!

Cut the deck so the Chosen Card is on TOP. Then *turn the deck over* and hold it in your hand as shown. The Chosen Card is now on the bottom.

Have the Spectator *STRIKE* the cards *SHARPLY!* All the cards will fall to the floor except for the Chosen Card which you will be still gripping in your hand! *TRY IT!*

CHAIR FARE!

Cut the deck so the Chosen Card is on top. Fan the cards, FACE DOWN, and start pulling cards out of the middle, letting them fall to the floor. AS SOON AS ONE FALLS FACE DOWN - STOP. Say: "That is your card!"

When the Spectator reaches down to pick up the card, he will lean forward in his chair. Quickly, and secretly, place the Chosen Card on his seat! Of course, the spectator finds that the card on the floor is not his card. Both of you look through the deck and find the card is MISSING. Ask the Spectator to stand and say:

"No *wonder* I couldn't find it... You were *SITTING* on it!"

FLOWERS
CARD TRICK

This magical ending *looks* impossible and will leave your audience *baffled!*

Cut the deck so the Chosen Card is on top. Then place the cards *FACE DOWN* on the table to form 5 FLOWERS.

You *KNOW* which face down card is the Chosen Card. REMEMBER where it is!

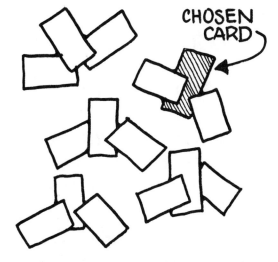

CHOSEN CARD

Ask the Spectator to *POINT* at any 2 of the Flowers...

If they point to 2 Flowers that *DO NOT* include the Chosen Card, take them away. *BUT* If they point to 2 Flowers that *INCLUDE* the Chosen Card, take the *OTHER* 3 away so the Chosen Card is still there!

Ask the Spectator to *POINT* to 2 of the remaining Flowers. If they point to 2 Flowers that *DO NOT* include the Chosen Card, take them away. If they point to 2 Flowers that include the chosen card, take the *OTHER FLOWER* away!

➡ DO THIS UNTIL THERE IS ONLY ONE FLOWER LEFT. It is the Flower that has the Chosen Card. Spread out the 3 'petals'. Ask the Spectator to *POINT* to 2 of the petals. If the 2 petals *DO NOT* include the Chosen Card, take them away. If they *DO INCLUDE* the Chosen Card, take the *OTHER* card away, and ask him to *POINT* to one of the remaining cards. Take away the card that is *NOT* the chosen Card.

THERE IS ONE CARD LEFT! It is the *CHOSEN CARD.* Ask the Spectator to turn it over and you will have fun watching his AMAZEMENT! *He has been tricked......*

This Final *Magical Ending* for a card trick is funny and simple to do.

I BET

You don't have to *CUT THE DECK*. You can leave the Chosen Card where it rests in the middle.

Turn over the cards, one by one until you see the Chosen Card. *DON'T PAUSE!* Keep turning over 4 or 5 more cards. *THEN STOP...* Keeping your hands on the deck *SAY*:

"I bet you the *NEXT CARD I TURN OVER* is the card you chose."

Of course, the spectator can see that you have *already* turned over his card so he will be happy to accept your bet!

Now you reach out, pluck the Chosen Card from its place and turn it *OVER* onto its *FACE!*

REMEMBER

If you used the KEY CARD method, the Chosen Card is the one that turns up after the KEY CARD. If you used the PICTURE BOOK method, the Chosen Card will be the first *Reversed Card*.

HAVE FUN WITH THESE CARD TRICKS!

join the CLUB

You and your friends can start a CARD CLUB! Maybe you will want to meet once a week and play CARD GAMES!

You can take turns meeting at each other's homes. All you really NEED is a DECK of CARDS and paper and pencils for SCORING.

A CARD CLUB WOULD BE FUN!

IDEAS FOR CLUB NAMES
JACK of CLUBS
JOKER'S WILD
ROYAL DIAMOND
HOUSE of CARDS

♣ BOARD of DIRECTORS ♣

MEMBERSHIP CHAIRPERSON
keeps lists of members and phone numbers.

SITE SUPERVISOR
Finds places to meet

HOSPITALITY CHAIRPERSON
In charge of SNACKS!

OFFICIAL SCOREKEEPER
keeps track of how many games each person has won...

TREASURER
keeps track of club money. You can each put in a quarter every time you meet or you can make money collecting bottles and stuff!

CHAMPIONSHIPS
You can have a TROPHY for the member who wins the most games in a month. Or, you can have a TROPHY for some of the WINNERS on the next page!

MAKE A TROPHY!
It is EASY to make trophies out of stuff from around the house! little boxes · tin foil milk cartons · tape cardboard tubes · glue old cards.

SNACKS
You can take turns bringing snacks or if you have club money you can buy snacks with it... PEANUTS · RAISINS POPCORN · CHIPS FRUIT · JUICE

ACE OF CLUBS

WINNERS!

In every sport, there may be lots of people playing but there can be only ONE winner of each game...

BUT WAIT! There is more to a game than having the winning score! AND, there many different kinds of WINNERS. Many sports offer prizes to these kinds of WINNERS!

★ MOST CONGENIAL PLAYER
This WINNER is fun to play with. They smile and laugh a lot and try not to hurt anyone's feelings. They are polite and don't start fights.

★ THE GOOD SPORT AWARD

These WINNERS do not get upset when they are losing! Even if they are in last place, they always play their best and don't spoil the game. The GOOD SPORT knows that we play games FOR FUN!

★ PLAYER OF THE DAY
This award goes to someone who did something very SPECIAL, like correcting a scoring error even though it made their score less! Or, gave in to a debate without starting a fight. Or, solved a problem in a way that was fair to everyone. Or shared something. Or helped someone!

These kinds of winners are VERY IMPORTANT! They help people feel good and have fun! When this happens, in a way, EVERYBODY IS A WINNER!

WHIST GAME

WHIST is a very old and very popular kind of card game. There are many different WHIST games that you can learn. People play whist in clubs or in tournaments, as well as at home with their friends!

You will enjoy WHIST and it is VERY easy to learn, but never gets boring.

WHIST IS KIND OF LIKE THE GAME of WAR, SO YOU WILL NEED TO REMEMBER the KINGDOM of CARDS.

A MAGIC KINGDOM

A K Q J 10 9 8 7 6 5 4 3 2

The ACE is the highest card in a suit. The KING is the next highest. Then the QUEEN, the JACK and so on down to the little TWO.

There are 4 SUITS.

♣ ♦ ♡ ♠
CLUBS   DIAMONDS   HEARTS   SPADES

Each suit has all 13 cards shown above.

basic WHIST

Before you learn some of the many WHIST GAMES, you must understand the *basic* way all of them are played.

To start, choose a dealer. Deal all the cards so that everyone has the same number. If there are cards left over, just put them to the side.

Most WHIST games have their own special deal. To learn the basics of WHIST, for now we will just deal out the whole deck. If there are 4 players, each will have 13 cards.

ALWAYS DEAL TO THE LEFT

TAKE TURNS BEING DEALER

Players hold their cards in their hands so that no one else can see them!

Its a good idea to sort the cards INTO SUITS. Put the ♡s together, the ♤s together, the ♢s together and the ♧s together.

If you can, FAN OUT THE CARDS in your hands so that you can see them all!

THE PLAY at WHIST!

The player to the LEFT of DEALER goes FIRST.

He chooses a card from his hand and plays it *FACE UP*, in the middle of the table.

This is called the **LEAD** and the 1st player is called the **LEADER**.

The person LEFT of the LEADER plays the next card. The person on his LEFT plays the next. This goes on around the table...

When everyone has played *ONE CARD EACH*, the *HIGHEST CARD* wins the PILE!

THIS PILE IS CALLED A **TRICK**

The winner of the TRICK gathers up the pile and puts it in front of him. Now, <u>that</u> person is the LEADER. THE WINNER OF A TRICK PLAYS THE NEXT LEAD!

After all the cards are played, COUNT THE NUMBER OF TRICKS YOU HAVE WON!

3rd card

2nd card

4th card

LEFT

THE LEADER 1st card

PILE YOUR TRICKS LIKE THIS SO THEY ARE EASY TO COUNT LATER.

FOLLOW the LEADER

In WHIST games, the card you play on a TRICK must be the SAME SUIT as the card that was LED.

If the LEADER plays a ♡ card, everyone must play a ♡ card. If the LEAD was a ♣ card, everyone must play a ♣ card. The same for ♠s and ◇s.

The LEADER picks the SUIT. Everyone else *MUST FOLLOW SUIT IF THEY CAN!*

BUT WHAT IF I HAVE NO CARDS IN THAT SUIT?

If you have NO CARDS in the suit that was LED, you will have to play a card from another suit.

BUT

YOU CANNOT WIN the TRICK, even if the card you played is the HIGHEST on the PILE!

The HIGHEST CARD in the SUIT THAT was LED wins the TRICK.

There is, however, a SPECIAL SUIT in WHIST. This suit is called THE TRUMP SUIT.

Read on!

TRUMP!

At the beginning of each DEAL, you pick a suit to be the *TRUMP SUIT*.

IF YOU DON'T HAVE ANY CARDS IN THE SUIT THAT WAS LED YOU CAN PLAY A CARD FROM *the TRUMP SUIT!*

A TRUMP CARD IS HIGHER than any card in any other suit!

TRUMP CARDS WIN TRICKS

➡️ The only time a TRUMP CARD does *NOT* win the trick is when someone else plays a HIGHER trump.

⭐ You can play a TRUMP SUIT card anytime, but *ONLY* if you have *NO CARDS* in the suit LED.

⭐ You don't HAVE to play a TRUMP CARD if you don't *want to*....

⭐ Anyone can LEAD a TRUMP SUIT CARD if they want to! When a TRUMP is LED, everyone MUST play a TRUMP. The highest one *WINS the TRICK!*

PICKING THE TRUMP SUIT

Every game of WHIST has its own way of picking what suit will be TRUMP. For *basic whist* simply CUT the DECK and turn over the top card. That suit will be TRUMP for the next DEAL.

SCORING

Basic WHIST is kind of a *PRACTICE GAME* to help you learn how to play. The *other* games of whist you will learn in this book each have their own way of SCORING. If you want to keep score at *basic whist* simply count your tricks at the end of each DEAL.

PUZZLE PAGE

WHAT DO YOU KNOW about WHIST?

If ♡s are TRUMP, which card won each of these tricks?

     ① ANSWER

LEAD

     ②

LEAD

     ③

LEAD

     ④

LEAD

     ⑤

LEAD

  ⑥

LEAD

ARE YOU A SMART CAT?

Try to answer these questions about WHIST!

1. The person who plays the FIRST card on the table is the _____

2. What do we call the pile of cards which has one card from each player? _____

3. Who is the LEADER for the NEXT TRICK?
_____
_____

4. In WHIST, there is a *special* suit. What is it called? _____

5. Which DIRECTION do people's turns go?
_____

Answers on page 102

PARTNERS

WHIST FOR 4 PLAYERS

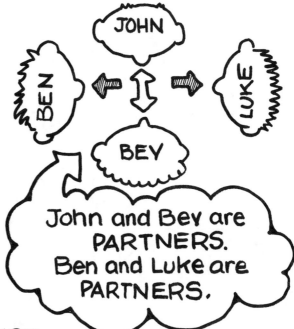

JOHN

BEN

LUKE

BEY

John and Bev are PARTNERS. Ben and Luke are PARTNERS.

PARTNER WHIST is one of the *best* games of Whist!

You and your PARTNER are a *TEAM* and sit across from each other. The other 2 players are also a *TEAM* and sit on either side of you.

THE PLAY in PARTNER WHIST is much the *same* as Basic Whist.

BUT The TRICKS your partner wins are counted for *YOUR TEAM*. At the end of each deal, your tricks and partner's tricks are *ADDED TOGETHER!*

the **DEAL**

DEAL OUT ALL THE CARDS. Deal to the LEFT. Deal the cards one by one, *FACE DOWN*.

Each player will have 13 cards. Hold your cards so that only you can see them. Sort your cards into suits.

the **play!**

The person to the LEFT of Dealer makes the first LEAD.

The winner of the TRICK is the next LEADER.

Players must *FOLLOW SUIT.*

If you have no cards in the suit that was LED, you can play a card from another suit (*which will never win a trick*) or you can play a TRUMP SUIT card which will win if it is the *HIGHEST TRUMP CARD* played on that trick.

What is **Trump** ?

♣s are TRUMP the 1st deal.
◇s are TRUMP the 2nd deal.
♡s are TRUMP the 3rd deal.
♤s are TRUMP the 4th deal.
NO TRUMP! The 5th deal is played with *NO TRUMP SUIT.*

After the No Trump deal you can end the game or you can start over with ♣s.

WE	THEY

the **SCORE**

The easiest way to SCORE is to simply count your team's tricks at the end of each DEAL. Write your total under 'WE' and write the other team's score under 'THEY.'

After 5 deals, add up the scores to see who is *WINNING* the game.
REMEMBER→ count YOUR tricks *and* partner's tricks for your SCORE.

TIPS

PARTNERS WHIST is challenging and fun. Here are a few helpful tips about playing with A PARTNER!

WINNING TRICKS

Remember that the tricks your *PARTNER* wins are *YOUR* tricks! If you see that the card your PARTNER played on a trick is the *HIGHEST,* you are happy. YOU DON'T HAVE TO TRY TO WIN THE TRICK IF PARTNER'S CARD IS GOING TO WIN! You can save your high card for another trick...

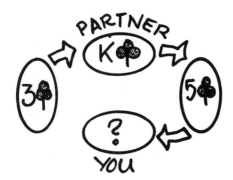

Here, you don't need to play your A of ♣ to win the trick. Partner has *already* won the trick for your TEAM! You can save your A♣ for play on another trick!

TRUMPS

If you know that PARTNER has NO CARDS in a suit, when it is your LEAD, you can lead *that suit,* so partner can *TRUMP* the trick and WIN it!

Let's say that *CLUBS* are TRUMP. You lead the A♡, partner played a ♢. You *KNOW* he has *NO* ♡s! Why did he NOT play a TRUMP? Because he sees that your A♡ will win *the TRICK!* and you are his *PARTNER.* Now, if you want, you can lead a little ♡ and partner can win the trick by *TRUMPING* - playing a TRUMP card on the trick.

Name each picture. Then take the FIRST LETTER of each name and print it in the right-numbered box or boxes at the bottom.

Answers on page 102

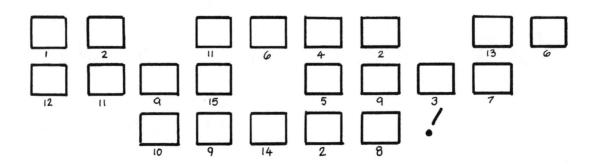

HONEYMOON

A WHIST GAME for 2 PLAYERS

Shuffle the deck and place it
FACE DOWN between you
and the other player.

You will play 5 DEALS. ♣s are
TRUMP the 1st DEAL. Then ♦s, then
♥s, then ♠s, then NO TRUMP. The 5th
deal is played with NO TRUMP SUIT.

the DEAL

Take Turns. The NONDEALER goes first.
During the DEAL, you are choosing cards
to make up your hand.

PICK UP the TOP CARD. If you WANT IT, KEEP IT and
THROW AWAY the next card. If you DON'T want the
1st card, THROW IT AWAY and TAKE the NEXT CARD!

YOU CAN'T CHANGE YOUR MIND. If you decide to
KEEP the 1st card, and throw away the next, you are
allowed to LOOK at the card you throw away, BUT you
are NOT ALLOWED TO CHANGE YOUR MIND! If you throw
away the 1st card you MUST take the 2nd – even if
you don't WANT IT!

Take turns doing this until the LAST 2 CARDS. The
person who gets the last 2 cards is allowed to
pick them both up, choose one, and throw the other away.

Of course, during the deal, you want to KEEP
TRUMP CARDS and High Cards in other suits!

the PLAY

After the DEAL you will each have 13 cards.

NONDEALER makes the First LEAD.

Each of you plays ONE CARD. YOU *MUST* play a card in the suit that was LED if you can.

If you have NO CARDS in the suit that was LED, you can play a card from another suit *(which will NEVER win!)* OR you can play a *TRUMP* card which will WIN the TRICK. *(If 2 TRUMP cards are played, the HIGHEST one WINS).*

THE HIGHEST CARD IN THE SUIT THAT WAS LED WINS. *OR* a player can win the TRICK by TRUMPING.

KEEP SCORE.
Write down the number of tricks you WON after each DEAL. At the end of 5 deals, the person who won the *MOST* tricks is the

Winner!

Remember to place your tricks like this so you can keep COUNT!

9-5-2

A WHIST GAME for 3 PLAYERS!

Shuffle the deck. Pick a Dealer. Deal 16 cards to each player. There will be 4 cards left over. Keep these cards FACE DOWN.

9-5-2 is a game where players win TRICKS, just like other WHIST games. Of course, you must FOLLOW SUIT if you can! The player to the LEFT of dealer is the LEADER and plays the first card.

9	5	2
THE DEALER MUST WIN 9 TRICKS	THE PLAYER ON DEALER'S LEFT MUST WIN 5 TRICKS	THE OTHER PLAYER MUST WIN 2 TRICKS

The object of playing 9-5-2 is to WIN the number of tricks you need PLUS MORE IF YOU CAN!

TAKE TURNS BEING DEALER. The person to the *left* of Dealer will be the NEXT Dealer.

DEALER PICKS THE *TRUMP SUIT!*

The Dealer looks at his hand and decides which suit will be TRUMP. *OR*, if he wants, Dealer can say there will be NO TRUMP.

HINT: The more trump cards you have, the better, so you should pick a suit in which you have lots of cards!

HMMM....
I THINK I'LL SAY
HEARTS ARE *TRUMP!*

AFTER HE ANNOUNCES THE TRUMP SUIT, DEALER PICKS UP THE *FOUR* CARDS....

Remember there were 4 left over from the deal! Dealer can add these cards to his hand, *BUT* must throw 4 away. He can throw away *any* 4 cards. These are put, *FACE DOWN*, to the side and are *NOT* counted in the play of this deal.

SCORE

CHUCK	JASON	ASHLEY
10	10	10

EACH PLAYER STARTS WITH 10....

Count the number of tricks you have won....

If you won EXACTLY the number of tricks you needed - *like 9 or 5 or 2 -* YOU SCORE *NOTHING.*

If you won *MORE*, *SUBTRACT* one point for each *EXTRA TRICK* from your score!

If you won *LESS*, ADD one point for each trick *LESS* to your score!

THE FIRST PERSON TO GET THEIR SCORE DOWN TO ZERO IS THE *WINNER!*

 HEARTS

A great Whist-like game for 3, 4, 5 or 6 players!

In HEARTS, players play cards and win tricks just like in Whist.

 **BUT ➡ YOU DON'T WANT HEARTS!**
You do *NOT* want to win a trick that has *any* ♡s in it!

At the end of each DEAL, the number of ♡s you won is counted and added to your SCORE. At the end of the game, the person with the *LOWEST SCORE* is the WINNER!

 **PLUS ➡ YOU DON'T WANT *the* QUEEN of ♠!**
This card is called the BLACK LADY. If you win this card on a trick, you will have 13 POINTS added to your SCORE!

IN THE PLAY it doesn't matter how many TRICKS you win. In fact, each time you win a TRICK, take out the ♡s or Q♠ and put them in front of you for *COUNTING* later. Throw all the rest of the cards into a discard pile, *FACE DOWN.*

the Deal

Play HEARTS with a regular deck. Before the DEAL, you may have to REMOVE some cards...

If there are 3 players, REMOVE the 2 of ♣.

If there are 5 players, REMOVE the 2 of ♣ and 2 of ◇.

If there are 6 players, REMOVE the 2 of ♣, 2 of ◇, 2 of ♠ and 3 of ♣.

Now the deck is ready. Shuffle it up and deal out ALL the cards, FACE DOWN. Each player will have the same number of cards.

THE pass

Before the PLAY starts, you do the PASS. Each player chooses 3 cards from their hand. Usually these are 3 cards that *they don't want!*

The 1ST DEAL, you PASS these cards, FACE DOWN, to the player on your LEFT. Then you pick up the 3 cards PASSED to you!

The 2ND DEAL, you PASS the 3 cards to the player on your RIGHT. The 3RD DEAL is a KEEPER. No one PASSES any cards.

AFTER the PASS, you start to play. The person to the LEFT of dealer makes the 1ST LEAD.

PLAYERS MUST FOLLOW SUIT if they can. The HIGHEST card played in the LEADER'S SUIT *WINS THE TRICK!* The WINNER of the TRICK is the *next* LEADER.

the DISCARD

If you have NO CARDS in the suit that was LED, you can play a card from *any other suit.* This will NEVER win the trick no matter what the card is!

Playing a card from *another suit* is called DISCARDING. You can DISCARD *anything you want* when you have NO CARDS in the suit that was LED.

 You may want to DISCARD a ♡! Then the person who wins that trick will HAVE TO WIN YOUR ♡!

 You may want to DISCARD the QUEEN of ♠s. Then the person who *wins* that trick will have to win the Q♠!

 You may want to DISCARD an Ace, King or Queen. You don't LIKE your high cards, because they *WIN TRICKS,* and if someone DISCARDS on *your* trick, you will have to win that ♡, or worse, the Q♠. You DON'T WANT TO WIN TRICKS! So you DISCARD your high cards when you get the chance. DISCARDS *never WIN!*

LEADING HEARTS

HEARTS MAY NOT BE LED ON THE FIRST LEAD (or TRICK).

After the 1st LEAD, anyone can lead ♡s when it is their turn to LEAD.

If you LEAD a HIGH HEART *(like the A, K, Q or J),* you will WIN the trick and all those ♡s will count against you! The other players will surely play *LOW* ♡s! Its a good idea *NOT* to lead ♡s unless you LEAD a VERY LOW ♡ *(like the 2, 3, 4 or 5).* Then someone *ELSE* will have to WIN it!

shoot the moon

IF YOU WIN ALL 13 HEARTS *and* THE QUEEN *of* SPADES, YOU SCORE ZERO POINTS *and* EVERYONE ELSE SCORES 26!

This is called *SHOOT THE MOON* (or sometimes *TAKE ALL*). Deciding to Shoot The Moon is *RISKY!* You will have to *WIN* ♡s which could count *against you* unless you are able to WIN THEM ALL.

If you plan to Shoot The Moon, it is best to *keep it a secret as long as you can!* The other players will happily DISCARD all their ♡s on your winning tricks BUT, if they know you are trying to *Take them All*, they will try to STOP you. They will all try to win at least one ♡ themselves!

A ♡
K ♡
Q ♡
J ♡
10 ♡
9 ♡
8 ♡
7 ♡
6 ♡
5 ♡
4 ♡
3 ♡
2 ♡
Q ♠

In order to *SHOOT THE MOON* and *WIN*, you need a hand that can WIN TRICKS. You need lots of Aces, Kings, and Queens. The best hand would have the AKQ of ♠ *and* the AKQJ *and more* ♡s!

THE Score!

Each GAME of ♡s is over after 3 DEALS. Before you start, you can agree on the number of GAMES you will play. Keep the SCORE until you are *finished playing*. Then, the LOWEST SCORE WINS!

EACH ♡ = 1 POINT Q♠ = 13 POINTS
13♡s + the Q♠ = 0 POINTS *and* everyone else *SCORES* 26 POINTS.

OLD CARDS

CARD TOSS!

Each person, in turn, throws a card at a wall. If the card lands on TOP of one or more of the other cards, the TOSSER wins them ALL. LEANERS win 3 cards. You will need to learn to FLICK the cards!

STOP! DON'T THROW THOSE CARDS AWAY!
There are LOTS of things you can do with those old cards!

LEANER!

TOSSER WINS all 3 cards

TOSSER WINS both cards

SIDE VIEW

CARD

FORK

MOTOR BIKE
You can make your bike sound like it has a motor! Use CLOTHES PEGS to clip OLD CARDS onto the FORKS.

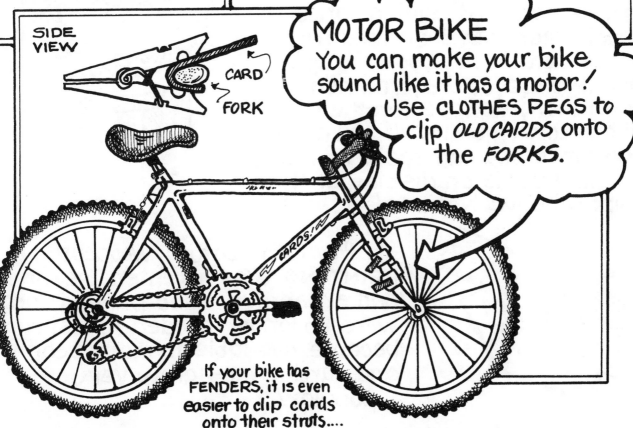

If your bike has FENDERS, it is even easier to clip cards onto their struts....

HISTORY of cards

Over 1000 years ago, in China, people were using a deck of playing cards that had 4 suits and 14 cards in each suit. Cards have been around a *LONG TIME!* Back then, they used cards for money as well as games.

Historians believe that when Marco Polo and his dad explored the Orient about 1269 AD, they discovered cards and brought them back to Europe.

In those days, of course, there were no printing presses so cards had to be each hand painted. In 1392, the French King Charles VI ordered 3 decks of hand-painted cards. The royal treasurer described them in his accounting book, "in gold and diverse colors, ornamented with many devices, for the diversion of our Lord, the King." If you are ever in France, you can see 17 of these original cards on display at the Bibliothèque Nationale.

In the 15th century, WOODCUT PRINTING was invented. The rare and expensive hand-painted cards were no longer needed. At last, cards became available to many people and card games grew very popular!

Today's cards look much the same as they did back in the 16th century. The HONOR cards are dressed in clothing worn by royalty during the Elizabethan period. The only real change in the modern deck is the placing of numbers in the corners and drawing the pictures to look the same upside down or rightside up. Look at your cards and you will see what this means!

Many of the old decks had an extra honor card called the Cavalier or Knight. Some also had 22 extra cards, each drawn in detail with lots of symbols from astrology, numerology and other old sciences. These decks were called TAROT cards and are still made today. The Tarot deck was, and still is, used for fortune telling. In the 'olden' days these cards were thought to be connected with witchcraft and many religions would not allow cards to be played. They called them the Devil's Picturebook. Also, in the early history of North America, cards became very popular in saloons and gambling dens. Good citizens believed that cards would lead to a bad life. With such a reputation, it is amazing that cards are still around!

Today, playing cards are widely accepted as a toy or amusement. The modern deck has only 3 honors in a suit and the 22 Tarot cards are gone. Card games are played all over the world and have become a wonderful way for people of all ages and backgrounds to enjoy each other's company!

ALL ALONE?

No one to play with?

cheer up

You don't need another person in order to play a card game... There are many card games for just

ONE PERSON

Sometimes it is hard to find someone to play cards.

but Don't be blue! You can play cards by yourself!

Card games for just one person are called

SOLITAIRE

Card lovers play SOLITAIRE when they are alone, when they are waiting for something or when they are bored. You can play SOLITAIRE anytime and any place. You can keep a personal score or just play for fun. SOLITAIRE is a GOOD way to pass the time.

WHAT IS A SEQUENCE

In most games of SOLITAIRE, you will be playing cards in SEQUENCE!

A SEQUENCE of cards are cards whose *NUMBERS* or *RANKING* are in order!

AN UPWARD SEQUENCE of cards is one that starts *LOW* and goes *HIGHER*, just like counting forwards.

A 2 3 4 5 6 7 8 9 10 J Q K

A DOWNWARD SEQUENCE of cards is one that starts *HIGH* and goes *LOWER*, just like counting backwards.

K Q J 10 9 8 7 6 5 4 3 2 A

CARD SEQUENCES in SOLITAIRE GAMES *always* count the ACE as the LOWEST CARD and the KING as the HIGHEST CARD!

A 2 3 4 5 6 7 8 9 10 J Q K Q J 10 9 8 7 6 5 4 3 2 A

UPWARD

DOWNWARD

SEQUENCE HILL

TIME OUT

Take time out from your busy day and play a game of SOLITAIRE. TIME OUT is a special game that is designed to help you learn how many SOLITAIRE games work...

Use a standard deck of 52 cards. Take out the 4 Aces and place them in the middle of the table. Like this ➡

These 4 Aces are called the...

FOUNDATION

Shuffle the rest of the deck. Deal out the 4 top cards and place them in a row FACE UP. ➡

These cards are called the...

TABLEAU

The rest of the cards, FACE DOWN, make up the STOCK. Turn one FACE UP to start the DISCARD PILE.

STOCK *face down*

DISCARD *face up*

76

In this game, you want to
BUILD
onto the FOUNDATION by moving cards from the TABLEAU, or the STOCK, or the DISCARD PILE, up to the FOUNDATION piles.

Cards moved to the FOUNDATION must be the same SUIT as the Ace *and* the cards must 'build' in a LOW to HIGH SEQUENCE. A 2 3 4 5 6 7 8 9 10 J Q K

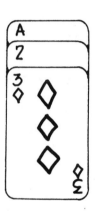

FOUNDATION

TABLEAU

Building on your FOUNDATION is the *KEY* to playing this game. If you complete all 4 piles you have

WON!
the game...

You can also build on the TABLEAU. These cards must go in a HIGH to LOW order. K Q J 10 9 8 7 6 5 4 3 2 *AND* they must go Black, red, black, red. They must *alternate* colors.
♠♣ are black
♡♢ are red.

Needs a
RED 5

Needs a
BLACK 9

Needs a
BLACK 7

Move this card up to the FOUNDATION

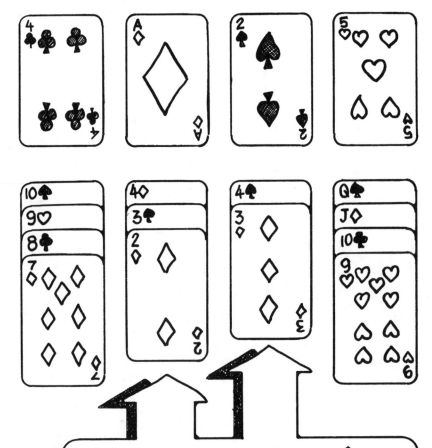

the FOUNDATION cards can be made into piles. You only need to see the Top card to know what card comes next.

the TABLEAU cards should be spread out so you can see them all.

Only cards from the TOP of a *tableau* pile may be moved up to the FOUNDATION. The cards underneath are FROZEN until you can FREE them.

You want to move that 3♠ up to the 2♠ but it is FROZEN. So, FREE it by moving up the 2◇ to the A◇. Now move up the 3♠ *and LOOK!* You can now move up the 3◇ (to the 2◇), the 4♠ (to the 3♠) and the 4◇ (to the 3◇). You have moved up all the cards from these two TABLEAU piles. Fill the spaces with cards from the DISCARD PILE!

Cards from the DISCARD pile can be used to fill in spaces, or to build onto the TABLEAU or FOUNDATION. *ONLY THE TOP CARD* may be used. The card under it is FROZEN until the top card is used.

If all the cards in the DISCARD PILE are used up, or you can't make any building plays with the top card, you can get a NEW card from the STOCK. Put this card FACE UP on top of the DISCARD PILE.

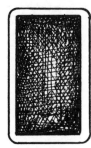

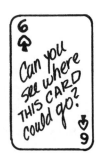

Can you see where THIS CARD could go?

STOCK   DISCARD

Move this BLACK 7, and all the cards above it, over to the RED 8.

10♥	Q♠	7♠	K♣
9♣	J♦	6♥	Q♥
8♦	10♣	5♣	J♠
		4♥	

TABLEAU NOW LOOKS LIKE *THIS!*

10♥	Q♠		K♣
9♣	J♦		Q♥
8♦	10♣		J♠
7♠			
6♥			
5♣			
4♥			

Space

NOW you have a *SPACE* that you can fill with a card from the DISCARD (or STOCK) PILE!

Can you see another move you could make now?

YES! You can move the 10♥, and all the cards on top, over to the BLACK J of ♠! making *another space!*

The TABLEAU cards can also move from one TABLEAU PILE to the other, as long as they are in the *right order and color.*

You can even take a card from the *MIDDLE* of a Tableau Pile!

BUT you must also take ALL the cards that are on TOP of it...

If you look at the example, you can see how we moved the BLACK 7 over to the RED 8, *taking with it all the cards on top!* (the 6♥, 5♣ and 4♥)

Moving whole rows like this is good because it helps create *SPACES.*

You can *FILL* these *SPACES* with cards from your DISCARD PILE, *or* your STOCK PILE.

In the game TIME OUT, you can only go through your STOCK PILE once!

STOCK   DISCARD

ITS A GOOD IDEA to use your DISCARD PILE whenever you can! The cards in the DISCARD PILE are *FROZEN* except for the card on TOP. Every time you move that TOP card, to the TABLEAU or FOUNDATION, you are *FREEING* the card below it!

Only use your STOCK PILE when there is *NO OTHER PLAY!* If you use up your STOCK PILE too soon you will have too many cards FROZEN in your DISCARD PILE!

BUILD

onto the FOUNDATION Aces with cards from the TABLEAU *or* DISCARD PILES. FOUNDATION cards must be in an *upward sequence* and the same suit. (A 2 3 4 5...)

BUILD

onto the TABLEAU with cards from the DISCARD PILE. If you are able to, you can also build on one TABLEAU pile with cards from another. TABLEAU cards must be in a *downward sequence* and must change colors as they go. (RED BLACK RED or BLACK RED BLACK)

PRACTICE GAME For your first game of TIME OUT do this:

When the stock pile is used up, turn over the DISCARD PILE and start a new STOCK PILE!

KLONDIKE

If you have ever seen anyone play SOLITAIRE, they were probably playing KLONDIKE. This game became popular during the *GOLD RUSH* days when the miners would spend their time *and* their gold in casinos and gaming rooms!

Even today, this game is played in *CASINOS*. Players pay $52 for the deck. When the game is over, they win $5 for each card on the FOUNDATION PILES.

KLONDIKE IS PLAYED LIKE TIME OUT but IT STARTS OUT DIFFERENTLY *and* THERE ARE MORE TABLEAU PILES TO BUILD UPON!

TO START DEAL the TABLEAU. Deal one FACE UP card then 6 *FACE DOWN*, across the table. Then, on the same piles, deal one Face up card on the 2nd pile, and 5 face down. Then one face up on the 3rd pile, and 4 face down. Keep dealing in this way until you deal one face up card on the last pile. Look at the drawing to see how the Tableau looks.

When the DEAL is *OVER*, put the rest of the cards, *FACE DOWN*, in a pile in front of you. This is your STOCK.

LOOK!

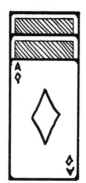

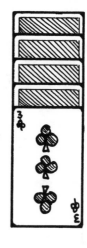
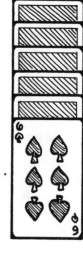
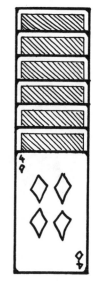

KLONDIKE TABLEAU

Here you can see how the DEAL turns out. You can 'square' up the piles so only the FACE UP cards are showing.

You can BUILD onto the TABLEAU using cards from your DISCARD PILE. You can also move cards from one TABLEAU PILE to another as long as you move *all the cards on top of the card you are moving* at the same time. Just like in TIME OUT, cards played on the TABLEAU must be in DOWNWARD SEQUENCE *and* MUST CHANGE COLORS.

There are 2 different ways to turn over cards from the STOCK. You can choose which way you would like to play.

REGULAR KLONDIKE
Take off 3 cards and turn them FACE UP on your DISCARD PILE. You must play the TOP card in order to be able to play the next one. Once you finish the STOCK, turn over the DISCARD pile and *start again* – turning over 3 cards at a time!

CASINO KLONDIKE
Turn STOCK CARDS over *ONE AT A TIME*, placing them on TOP of the DISCARD pile. Use *only* the TOP card of the DISCARD pile. You may go through the STOCK *only once*. When it is gone, *DO NOT* turn over the DISCARD PILE!

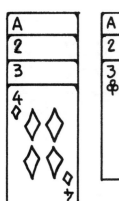

FOUNDATION

In order to start a FOUNDATION pile, an ACE must turn up as a TOP CARD on either the DISCARD pile or one of the TABLEAU piles. When an ACE turns up, move it to above the TABLEAU.

You BUILD onto the FOUNDATION piles with cards of the SAME SUIT as the Ace *and* in an UPWARD SEQUENCE!

A 2 3 4 5 6 7 8 9 10 J Q K ⟶

If you *COMPLETE ALL THE FOUNDATION PILES,* you have WON THE GAME! This doesn't happen very often. Usually, you play until there are no more moves. Then, count the number of cards on your FOUNDATION piles to see how well you have done!

FACE DOWN CARDS

You will notice there are a lot of FACE DOWN cards in the TABLEAU piles.

If one of these becomes a TOP card, you can turn it over and use it or build on it. Until then, these cards are FROZEN. Try to FREE them by moving cards from one TABLEAU PILE to another!

SPACES

When one of the TABLEAU PILES gets used up, you can fill the *SPACE* with any KING, but NO OTHER CARD! Use a King from the TOP of your DISCARD pile or move one over from another TABLEAU pile. Make sure you *also* move over any cards that are on TOP of that KING!

JOKER

All regular decks of playing cards come with two extra cards called JOKERS.

The picture on a Joker can be anything. It can be a horse, or the logo of the company that made the cards. MOST OFTEN, though, the JOKER has a drawing of a JESTER or ROYAL FOOL.

In the *Olden Days*, JESTERS were hired by Royal Families to keep them amused in their castles. Jesters would tell jokes, juggle, do magic tricks and generally make a *FOOL* out of themselves - like a *clown*.

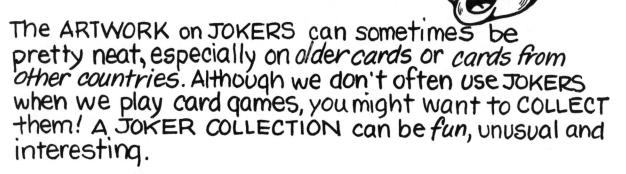

The ARTWORK on JOKERS can sometimes be pretty neat, especially on *older cards* or *cards from other countries*. Although we don't often use JOKERS when we play card games, you might want to COLLECT them! A JOKER COLLECTION can be *fun*, unusual and interesting.

Keep your JOKER COLLECTION in a photo album. Try to always write in the name of the Card Manufacturer *and* the date the cards were made if you can. If you have more than one of the same card, you can *TRADE* with your friends!

Spite And Malice!

♣ A CHALLENGE
SOLITAIRE GAME
for TWO ♠

You need 2 decks
and all 4 JOKERS.

deal

Shuffle ONE deck *without* the JOKERS.
Deal 26 to each player.
Keep this pile FACE DOWN to your left.
This is your STOCK.

Shuffle the 2nd deck, *with* the 4 JOKERS.
Deal 5 cards to each player.
This is your HAND.
Put the rest of this deck between you,
  off to one side a bit.
This is called the **PLAYERS' PILE.**

In this game, there will be a FOUNDATION.
  You will build on the FOUNDATION starting
  with Ace, then 2,3,4, and so on. SUITS DON'T
  MATTER! Foundation piles can have mixed
  suits. BOTH players can build on ANY
  FOUNDATION pile when it is their turn.

You will also each have 4 DISCARD
PILES. These piles are where you can
store your cards until they can be
used on a FOUNDATION pile. Only YOU
can put cards on your DISCARD PILE.

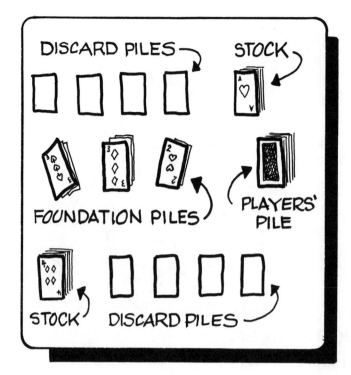

DISCARD PILES → STOCK →

FOUNDATION PILES → PLAYERS' PILE

STOCK → DISCARD PILES →

Turn up the TOP card of your STOCK PILE. These cards can be played ONLY on a FOUNDATION PILE.

The person who uses up her STOCK cards FIRST is the WINNER!

There can be as many as 8 FOUNDATION PILES at one time. When a FOUNDATION PILE is FINISHED, shuffle it into the PLAYERS' PILE.

At the beginning of each turn, take enough cards from the PLAYERS' PILE so you have 5 cards in your HAND.
    YOU MUST PLAY ANY ACES you have, to start new foundation piles. You must ALSO play ANY 2 if you can.

During your TURN, you try to use up your STOCK PILE by playing stock cards onto the foundation piles. If you use a stock card, turn up the next one. Only TOP cards may be used!

You can play cards from your HAND onto the FOUNDATION. You can play cards from you DISCARD PILES onto the FOUNDATION piles. You cannot play DISCARDS from pile to pile, only to the FOUNDATION: and you can only play a card from the TOP of a DISCARD PILE.

JOKERS are WILD. They can be any card EXCEPT AN ACE!

In one turn, you can keep playing your cards until there are no more moves. TO END YOUR TURN, you play a card from your hand onto one of your DISCARD PILES.

You can *START* your DISCARD PILES with *ANY CARD.* Once it is started, you may play *ONLY* cards that are in *DOWNWARD SEQUENCE* or you can play a card that is the *SAME RANK* as the top card. The SUIT DOESN'T MATTER.

DISCARD PILES

When choosing a DISCARD, try not to BURY cards you will need for play at your next turn. REMEMBER— only the TOP CARD may be used!

Sometimes, you will not be able to PLAY any cards, or DISCARD. When this happens, you are said to be FROZEN. When you are FROZEN, the *other* player keeps taking turns until you have a play.

If both players are FROZEN, all FOUNDATION piles, DISCARD piles, the PLAYERS' pile and both your hands are shuffled together. DO NOT shuffle in the STOCK piles! New hands are then dealt and PLAY starts over.

If you use up all 5 cards in your HAND *before* making a discard, you can pick up 5 new cards and *keep on playing!*

If the PLAYERS' PILE runs out and there are no completed FOUNDATION piles to shuffle up, shuffle all the FOUNDATION piles together for a new PLAYERS' PILE.

You DO NOT HAVE TO PLAY CARDS if you don't *want to!* EXCEPT— you *MUST PLAY* Aces and twos.

PEARS

GOT A MINUTE? Here is a QUICK and FUN little game of SOLITAIRE! (for one)

Start by dealing cards in a ROW, FACE UP, from left to right.

Whenever a card is dealt that MATCHES the RANK of another FACE UP card, deal another card, FACE UP, on top of EACH OF THE MATCHING CARDS.

Cover ANY TWO matching cards with two new cards, dealt FACE UP!

These 2 cards MATCH IN RANK. Cover them with 2 FACE UP cards from the deck!

DO NOT DEAL MORE THAN 8 CARDS IN THE ROW! If your FACE UP cards do not match up, you can add a new card to the right of the row, BUT you cannot have more than 8 PILES in the row. If you have 8 piles and none of the FACE UP cards match, the game is OVER!

IF YOU USE UP ALL THE CARDS IN THE DECK, YOU HAVE WON! If you have no more cards to deal, you have WON THE GAME.... YAY!

A FAST! CARD GAME FOR TWO PEOPLE

SPEED

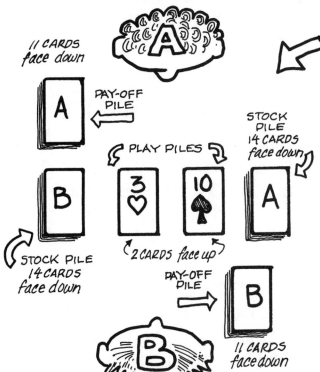

A

11 CARDS face down

A — PAY-OFF PILE

B

STOCK PILE 14 CARDS face down

PLAY PILES

3 ♥   10 ♠

2 CARDS face up

STOCK PILE 14 CARDS face down

A

PAY-OFF PILE → B

11 CARDS face down

B

Deal the cards as shown in the diagram.

THE OBJECT of the GAME is to be the *FIRST* person to use up all the cards in your PAY-OFF PILE!

To start, each player takes 3 cards from his PAY-OFF PILE. This is your *hand*. Use up these cards by BUILDING onto *EITHER* of the PLAY PILES - playing cards in SEQUENCE to the TOP card.

You can BUILD in SEQUENCE either UP or DOWN. *OR*, you can build up then down then up again. Suits do NOT matter! The Ace will take a 2 or a King The 3, a 2 or a 4.

At the beginning, someone says GO! BOTH PLAYERS PLAY AT THE SAME TIME!

Each time you play a card, you can pick one up from the PAY-OFF pile so your hand *always* has 3 cards -*never more!*

When the play STOPS because no one can make a play, you each turn over a STOCK card and place it on the PLAY PILES. Then say GO! again and *PLAY! PLAY! PLAY!*

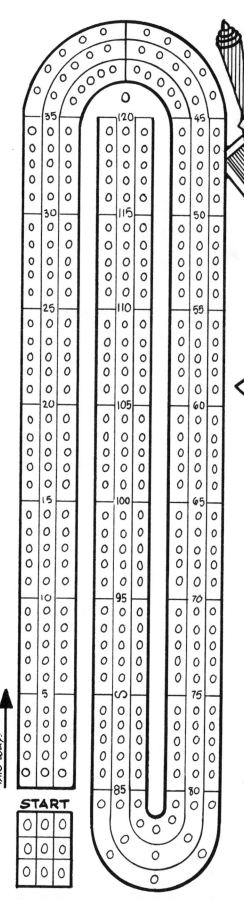

CRIB

CRIB is a *CARD GAME* for 2, 3, or 4 (partners) players. It is actually called CRIBBAGE, but we say CRIB, for short!

During the PLAY of CRIB, the players score points. The first person to score 121 points *WINS!*

Crib Board

Although the CRIB BOARD may *look* complicated, it is just a way to keep track of the score. You can play without a Board, but you would have to do a *lot* of adding!

Each player has 3 PEGS. These pegs fit into the holes on the Board. Each time you score points, you move a PEG forward, counting one hole for each point.

This is called *PEGGING.*

Pick a color and a row. When you are Pegging, *stay in your row!* Often the Crib Board will have each row a different color. There are 3 rows - the *outside*, the *middle* and the *inside* rows.

Start by putting your 3 pegs in *your row* in the START BOX.

All About 'PEGGING'

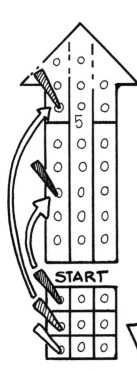

You will use *ONLY* your 2 front PEGS for *SCORING* or *PEGGING*.

The first time you score points, move the FRONT PEG forward, counting one point for each hole.

After that, *always move the BACK PEG forward*, counting one point for each hole *PAST the FRONT PEG!*

This drawing shows how PEGGING works. The first points scored were 3 so the FRONT peg moved up 3 holes. The next score was *also* 3, so the BACK peg moved up 3 holes *past the front peg!* Using 2 pegs like this helps you keep track of how many points you just scored.

The Crib Board is marked with numbers, counting by 5s. Every 5 holes (or points) the total is marked. The *END* of the board is marked 120. *BUT* you must score 121 (or more) to *WIN*. The 121st hole is at the very end and is usually marked with an *arrow*. If you get into this hole *first*, you WIN. You don't have to score *exactly* 121, you can score more. 121 or more will get you into that *last hole*.

Your 3rd PEG sits in the START box until you have won a game.

Then you can move it into the GAME box. This row keeps track of how many GAMES you have won...

How to Play CRIB

Now that you know *all about Pegging*, it is time to learn how the game of CRIB is played!

If you DON'T know all about Pegging, you'd best go back 2 pages and find out!

CRIB can be played with 2 or 3 people. Or, with 4 people playing as 2 sets of partners. Here you will learn to play with TWO PEOPLE. Later we will explain any changes for 3 or 4.

PICK A DEALER. Each of you cut the deck and show the bottom card. *LOWEST CARD* is 1st Dealer. After that, you *TAKE TURNS* being Dealer. Dealer shuffles the deck, the NONdealer cuts. Use a regular deck of 52 cards with *No Jokers.*

DEAL 6 CARDS to each player. Look at your hand and pick 2 cards to *PUT ASIDE.* When each of you has put aside 2 cards, there will be a pile of 4 cards. This is called the CRIB hand, or just the CRIB. Any points in the CRIB are scored *for the dealer!* The CRIB is left, *FACE DOWN,* until after the PLAY of this hand is over.

CUT the DECK. NONdealer now *CUTS* the rest of the deck. Dealer turns over the TOP CARD. After the PLAY, when you are counting your hand, you will add this TOP CARD to the rest of your cards!

IF the TOP CARD is a JACK, DEALER *SCORES 2 POINTS!*

There are 2 PARTS to the game of CRIB. You can score points in each part!

PART ONE *is The PLAY*
PART TWO *is The COUNT*

the play

Crib is an *ADDING* game. You play your cards, one by one, *FACE UP* in front of you. You can make your own little pile, but don't mix your cards with the other player's!

NONDEALER goes first. Play ONE card and *call out its VALUE.*

ACEs *equal* ONE *and* K, Q, J *or* 10 *equal* TEN
the OTHER CARDS *equal* THEIR NUMBER
9 EQUALS 9   8 EQUALS 8   7 EQUALS 7   6 EQUALS 6   AND SO ON...

DEALER then plays a card and, *adding it to yours,* calls out the *TOTAL.* Then you play a another card and, *adding it to the TOTAL,* call out the *New TOTAL.* This goes on, each of you *taking turns* playing a card and *adding its value* to the TOTAL.

DO NOT GO PAST 31! You cannot add to a total of more than 31. If you have no card to play without adding past 31, you must say

GO!

If you play a card that makes the *TOTAL* exactly 31, then you SCORE TWO POINTS!

You say "31 for 2" and move your BACK PEG 2 holes past your FRONT PEG!

SCORING *during the* PLAY

If you play a card that makes the *TOTAL 31* you SCORE 2 POINTS.
If you play a card that makes the *TOTAL 15* you SCORE 2 POINTS.
If you play a card that makes a certain *COMBINATION* of cards, here is what you SCORE (or PEG):

A PAIR *PEGs 2* → If you play a card that is the same RANK as the *last card played*, you score 2 points.

3 of A KIND *PEGs 6* → If you play a card that is the same RANK as the *last 2 cards played*, you score 6 points.

4 of A KIND *PEGs 12* → If you play a card that is the same RANK as the last *3 cards played*, you score 12 points!

These are cards of the same RANK. K must pair K, Q must pair Q, and so on. *JJJ or 77 or KKK*

THE RUN If you play a card that is in *SEQUENCE* with the last 2 or more cards, it is called a RUN. You will score 1 POINT for each card in the RUN.

It does not matter what *ORDER* the cards of the RUN are in, as long as they could be arranged into a sequence. 567 the person who played the 7 would score 3. 576 the person who played the 6 pegs 3. 579 NO *RUN* here! 5768 scores 4 points! PLUS, a RUN can be scored more than once! After one person scores 3 for 576, if the other *adds* to the RUN with an 8 or a 4, he would score 4 points!

the RUN must be 3 or more cards. Suits don't matter *and of course* you can't pass 31 in total!

If you cannot play a card without adding past 31, you say 'GO".

When one player says GO the other must play ALL the cards she can, but cannot pass 31.

If she plays a card that makes the total 31, she scores 2 points. *Otherwise, she scores ONE POINT for the GO.*

After a 'GO', if the other player plays cards that form a PAIR or a RUN or 3 of a KIND or 4 of a KIND, she scores points even if they are mostly her cards!

After one player says 'GO', if the other can't play any more cards, she takes her 1 POINT *'for the GO'* and the PLAY starts over again at ZERO.

WHENEVER *NEITHER PLAYER* CAN PLAY A CARD, *the* PLAY STARTS OVER *at* ZERO. The person who starts the play again is the one *OPPOSITE* the person who *played the LAST card.*

George played a card that made the total 29. Sally couldn't play a card so she said 'GO'. George couldn't play a card but he pegged one point for the 'GO'. Now the play starts over at ZERO. George played the *last card,* so SALLY starts the new PLAY.

RUNS, PAIRS, 3 of a KIND *or* 4 of a KIND *DO NOT COUNT* if they are interrupted by a GO *and* everything starts over!

the count!

The PLAY is *OVER* when no one has any cards left to play. Pick up your cards and get ready to *COUNT!*

NONDEALER *COUNTS FIRST!* Then the Dealer, then the CRIB. (Remember the CRIB counts for the Dealer). Who counts *FIRST* is IMPORTANT! When you are getting close to the end, the player who counts first gets first chance to reach the LAST HOLE, *121!*

Look at YOUR 4 cards PLUS the one on TOP of the deck and *COUNT POINTS* for each of the following:

FIFTEEN	Count 2 points each time 2 or more of your cards add up to 15.
PAIRS 3 of A KIND 4 of A KIND	Count 2 points for each PAIR. Count 6 for 3 cards of the same RANK. Count 12 for 4 cards of the same RANK.
FLUSH	4 cards of the *SAME SUIT* in your hand scores 4. 5 cards of the *SAME SUIT* (the 4 in your hand plus the one on the deck) counts for 5 points. 4-card flushes in the CRIB *do not count!* BUT, a 5-card flush (the CRIB plus the card on the deck) *DOES* count for 5 points.
HIS NIBS	Count 1 point if you have a JACK in the same suit as the card on the deck.
RUNS	Count 1 point FOR EACH CARD in a RUN of 3 or more cards.

After you have counted your hand up, move your peg forward the total number of points you counted!

Helpful Hints *about* counting

COUNT YOUR 15s FIRST!
Count 2 for each combination that adds up to 15. *THEN,* start counting pairs and runs and stuff like that...

FIFTEEN It is easier to count your 15s if you remember 3 MAIN Combinations:

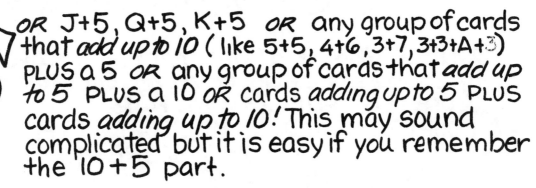

OR J+5, Q+5, K+5 OR any group of cards that *add up to 10* (like 5+5, 4+6, 3+7, 3+3+A+3) PLUS a 5 OR any group of cards that *add up to 5* PLUS a 10 OR cards *adding up to 5* PLUS cards *adding up to 10!* This may sound complicated but it is easy if you remember the 10+5 part.

OR cards *adding up to 9* PLUS a 6
OR cards *adding up to 6* PLUS a 9
OR cards *adding up to 6* PLUS OTHER cards *adding up to 9!*

OR cards *adding up to 8* PLUS a 7
OR cards *adding up to 7* PLUS an 8
OR cards *adding up to 7* PLUS OTHER cards *adding up to 8!*

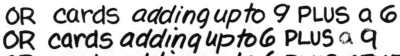

★ WATCH FOR THESE 3 COMBINATIONS ★

You can rearrange your cards to find *more* 15s.
 Do *NOT* count the same card *twice* in one 15!
 Do *NOT* count the same 15 *twice!*
Count OUT LOUD. Say "15-2" for your first 15, meaning 2 points, then "15-4" for the next 15, meaning 2 more points, then "15-6" and "15-8" and so on. The other player can check to see if you are right.

COUNTING RUNS

3 or more cards in a sequence is called a RUN. Count ONE POINT for each card in the RUN.

If one of the cards in a RUN is part of a PAIR then you actually have TWO RUNS!

| 5♡ 6♠ 7♡ |
| 5◇ 6♣ 7♡ |

A DOUBLE RUN is a RUN that has a PAIR in it, like 5567 or JKQQ or A223. Each RUN has 3 cards. Score 3+3 PLUS 2 for the PAIR

⇨ DOUBLE 3-CARD RUNS SCORE 8 POINTS!
⇨ DOUBLE 4-CARD RUNS SCORE 10 POINTS!
55678   10JQKK   A2234   Each RUN has 3 cards.

A TRIPLE RUN is a RUN that has 3 of a KIND in it. Like 888910 or 55567 or 23334. You have 3 RUNS, each worth 3 points. 8910 8910 8910 3+3+3 PLUS 6 POINTS for 3 of a KIND.

⇨ TRIPLE RUNS SCORE 15 POINTS!

A QUADRUPLE RUN is a RUN that has 2 PAIRS. Like 88910 10 or 55667 or JQQKK You have 4 RUNS, each with 3 cards. 567 567 567 567 3+3+3+3 PLUS 2 PAIR 2+2

⇨ A QUADRUPLE RUN SCORES 16 POINTS!

REMEMBER you are counting 5 cards! The 4 in your hand PLUS the one on top of the deck.

After everyone has counted and pegged, shuffle up the whole deck and start again!

and HAVE FUN!

Cribbage for 3 or 4

CRIB with 3 or 4 players is played the same way as Crib for 2, with a couple of changes.

═══ THREE PLAYER CRIB ═══

PEGGING : everyone has their own pegs and row.

THE DEAL : deal *ONLY 5 CARDS* to each player PLUS deal one card to the CRIB hand. Players choose *ONE* card to put in the CRIB hand.

THE 'GO' : The person to the LEFT of the 'GO' must play if able and if he does, the 3rd player must play if he can. This goes on until no one can play. The person who played the LAST CARD scores one point for the 'GO'. Then, the player on his LEFT starts the PLAY over at ZERO.

THE COUNT : Player to the LEFT of Dealer *COUNTS FIRST!*

═══ FOUR PLAYER CRIB ═══

CHOOSE PARTNERS ! Sit with partner *across* from you and the other players on either side. You and partner SCORE *ON THE SAME ROW*. Deal 5 cards to each. Everyone puts *ONE CARD* in the CRIB hand.

After a 'GO', players to the LEFT have turns to play. There may be more than one 'GO'! But only ONE POINT is scored 'for the go'. The person who played the *last card* scores the GO point. The person to his LEFT starts the PLAY over. Player to the *LEFT* of *DEALER* COUNTS FIRST.

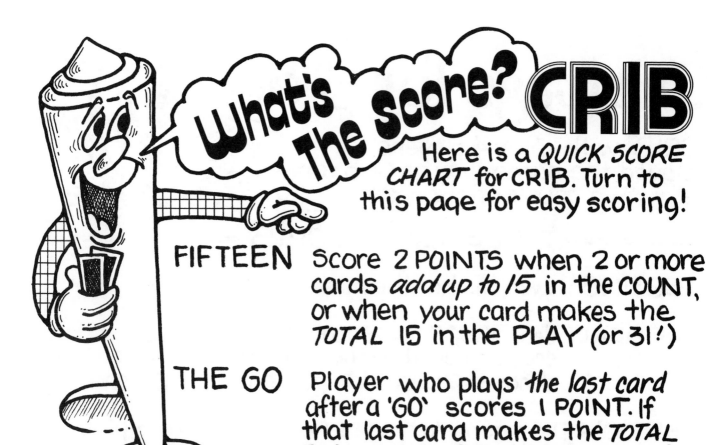

What's The Score? CRIB

Here is a *QUICK SCORE CHART* for CRIB. Turn to this page for easy scoring!

FIFTEEN — Score 2 POINTS when 2 or more cards *add up to 15* in the COUNT, or when your card makes the *TOTAL* 15 in the PLAY (or 31!)

THE GO — Player who plays *the last card* after a 'GO' scores 1 POINT. If that last card makes the *TOTAL* 31, it scores 2 POINTS, instead of 1.

A PAIR — Score 2 POINTS for a PAIR in the COUNT, or if you 'make' a PAIR in the PLAY.

3 of a KIND — Score 6 POINTS for 3 of a KIND in the COUNT, or if you 'make' 3 of a KIND in the PLAY.

4 of a KIND — Score 12 POINTS for 4 of a KIND in the COUNT, or if you 'make' 4 of a KIND in the PLAY.

A RUN — Score 1 POINT for each card in a RUN.

DOUBLE RUN	3-card run with a PAIR	SCORE 8 *
	4-card run with a PAIR	SCORE 10 *
TRIPLE RUN	a run with 3 of a KIND	SCORE 15 *
QUADRUPLE RUN	a run with 2 PAIRS	SCORE 16 *

* these RUNS include POINTS for PAIRS and 3 of a KIND! DON'T add them in twice!

HIS NIBS — Score 2 POINTS if the *turned up card* is a JACK and you are the DEALER.
Score 1 POINT if your hand (or crib) has the JACK in the *same suit* as the *turned up card*.

FLUSH

5 CARDS in the *Same Suit*	SCORE 5
4 CARDS in the *Same Suit*	SCORE 4

(in your hand, not in the CRIB.)

ANSWER PAGE

ROUND-UP (Page 8)

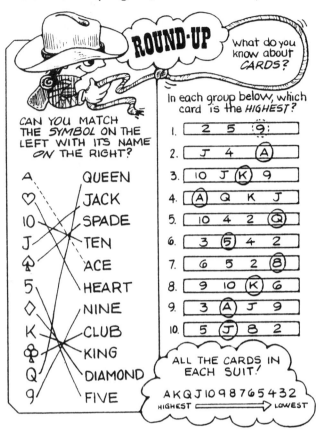

DOT TO DOT (Page 22)

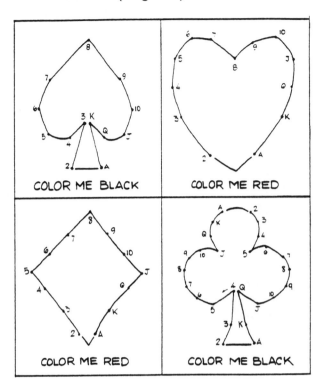

MAZE (Page 14)

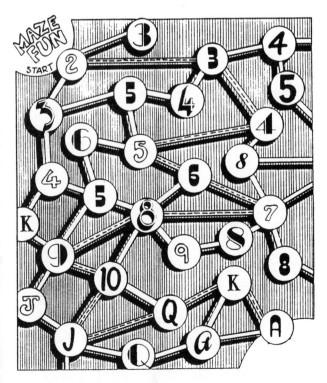

FIND A WORD (Page 26)

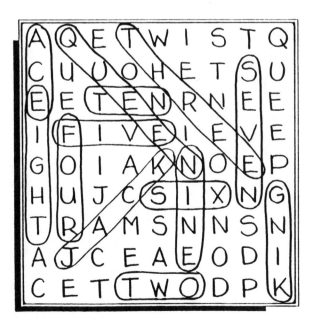

PUZZLE PAGE (Page 58)

1. ♡2   2. ♣Q   3. ♠A   4. ♡4   5. ♡A   6. ♣5

1. LEADER
2. A TRICK
3. THE PERSON WHO WON THE LAST TRICK
4. TRUMP
5. TO THE LEFT

PICTURE FUN (Page 62)

1. WHALE
2. EGG
3. RADIO
4. VACUUM CLEANER
5. CUP (OR COFFEE)
6. ORANGE
7. DESK
8. SANTA
9. AMBULANCE
10. GRAPE
11. LION
12. PAINT BRUSH
13. TREE
14. MOUSE
15. YARN

SOLUTION: KIDS LOVE TO PLAY CARD GAMES!

DEVYN PRESS PUBLICATIONS
BRIDGE BOOKS